STEPHANIE BARACH has taught piano for more than twenty-five years, including teaching assignments at the Washington College of Music, the Georgetown Settlement House, and Green Acres School. Her own musical training includes years of private instruction, leading to her acceptance in the Master's Class under Abram Chasins. She took her teacher's training under Lillian R. Wolfe. She has taught students of all ages, from preschool to adults, and is well known among Washingtonians as one of the city's leading instructors in piano.

PAUL HOFFMASTER is a Washington, D.C., artist and illustrator whose work has won prizes in Corcoran Gallery shows and whose illustrations have appeared in such magazines as the *National Geographic*, *Saturday Evening Post*, *Better Homes & Gardens*, *Nation's Business*, *U. S. News and World Report*, *Changing Times*, the *Kiplinger Magazine*, and *America Illustrated*.

PIERRE SALINGER who wrote the Introduction for this book, was Press Secretary to the President of the United States. He has been an accomplished pianist since boyhood.

An Introduction to the Language of Music

An Introduction to the Language of Music

by STEPHANIE BARACH

Robert B. Luce, Inc.
Washington, D.C.

AN INTRODUCTION TO THE LANGUAGE OF MUSIC

Published simultaneously in the Dominion of Canada

Second Printing September 1964

Library of Congress Catalog Card Number: 62-10216

MANUFACTURED IN THE UNITED STATES OF AMERICA

VAN REES PRESS • NEW YORK

To my husband,

ARNOLD

Introduction

By PIERRE SALINGER

Music means so much to me, has been such an integral part of my life, that I sometimes find it difficult to believe that there are those who have not shared this joy.

The vivid and happy memories of my youth revolve around music.

I can still see Sergei Rachmaninoff, standing solemnly on the stage of the San Francisco Civic Auditorium, following a series of concerts in which he had played all of his piano concertos. He was stern and unsmiling, bowing stiffly in response to the audience's thunderous ovation.

I remember my excitement at hearing George Gershwin play his *Rhapsody in Blue* and *Concerto in F* in the San Francisco Opera House, and my overwhelming happiness on being taken backstage to meet him. When Gershwin died at such an early age, I felt as though a loved member of my family had been taken from me.

I recall the delightful moments of conversation with the great conductor Pierre Monteux following his San Francisco concerts. I called him "Papa Pierre" and he called me "Little Pierre." Behind that walrus-like mustache and the bushy eyebrows, his eyes twinkled and his expressive face revealed the emotion and understanding which he pours into his music.

I can still see the staircase in my family's home, its walls lined with pictures of our famous guests: Pablo Casals, Enrico Caruso, Madame Schumann-Heink, Harold Bauer—musicians my father had brought to Salt Lake City when he took a brief fling at being an impresario.

I remember the disbelief with which I first heard the composer Henry Cowell play one of his strange-sounding piano compositions. I winced as he brought his arms crashing down on the keyboard to create a musical effect, or leaned into the piano and plucked the strings with his fingers. Today, as I listen to records of Cowell music, they sound tame and almost classical.

All this is to say that music can be a joy and a solace. It should be part of the fiber of life. I say "should be," because in too many American families it is not.

We are a proud nation with a proud cultural heritage. But because we have had the facts of European culture drummed into us with such regularity and effectiveness, we tend to underplay—and even downgrade—our own.

Worse than that: we have allowed the impression to grow that so-called "good" music is only for highbrows and intellectuals; that for young Americans to be practicing an instrument instead of playing Little League baseball is a demonstration of qualities which I can only describe as "un-red-blooded." And in this way, millions of our children miss out on something that could enrich their lives.

I am not advocating massive doses of good music for boys and girls. Nor do I wish to minimize what I consider a mighty contribution to music: American jazz. Our young people should come to appreciate the music played by Benny Goodman and Louis Armstrong or, in a more modern vein, Dave Brubeck. They will find they get more out of jazz if they have a solid foundation in classical music. Modern contrapuntal jazz is a direct throwback to Bach and Vivaldi, and enjoying the former can be greatly enhanced by understanding the latter.

Now I would like to personalize all this by telling you how I bring music into my own children's lives.

I consider them rather normal children. They like to play Little League baseball, and we have a tough time getting them to do their homework; they even, alas, like some of the worst of the current teen-age song hits. But in a kind of happy cooperative program we are giving them a foundation in good music by making music fun.

Two of my children play the piano—not well, but they enjoy it. My youngest boy plays the violin, and shows some talent. When I come home from work in the evening, we play good music on our record-player. During dinner, we sometimes have contests, and the kids try to figure out in which period a piece of music was written, who wrote it and, in exceptional cases, the actual name of the composition. It's a fine game, and they're all making progress. We try to make concert-going a family project, and when my youngest son, Stephen, plays in a musical competition, we all try to get there to hear him and give him some moral support. When musician friends of mine come to town, we invite them over for supper and let the children sit in on the conversation. You cannot spend three or four hours listening to Isaac Stern talk about music, culture in general, and the great needs of our country in these fields, without a little bit rubbing off on you. We all watch Leonard Bernstein conduct the New York Philharmonic on television—one of the great things television has done for this country.

This is taking good music, not in enormous doses, but in quantities that most young people can respond to. And I think the children will be the better for it.

As you have gathered, I'm for music! I feel sure that Stephanie Barach's INTRODUCTION TO THE LANGUAGE OF MUSIC will do something in this field; will contribute to an understanding of the language of this magnificent art form.

For music is a common thread that runs through lives all over the world. In a time of terrible strife, it can help to cut across the barriers that divide us. It is universal and it is unifying.

One need only read the reports of the Eastman Rochester Orchestra after its recent tour of the Soviet Union. They were wildly received, everywhere they went. And the basic reason was the excellence of their music. When I was in Moscow, the young American pianist Byron Janis played a concert and was called back for curtain calls thirty-one times!

So let all of us—young and old—try to make music a more important part of our lives—not just to prove that we are "cultured," but because we will enjoy it. It will mean something to us. It will bring us happiness. It will bring us peace. And it will bring us a greater understanding of the artistic ties that bind all men together.

PIERRE SALINGER

The White House
Washington, D. C., 1962

Preface

This book grew out of a need.

Along with most teachers of music, I have for many years felt the lack of a music dictionary or guide geared to the unique requirements of the beginner. Excellent volumes are available for the sophisticated musician and musicologist, both of whom have the necessary educational background in theory and music history to make good use of them. But few such books, in my experience, serve the particular demands of the child or adult in the early stages of his training.

My purpose has been to fill that need with a dictionary that includes the words and terms most likely to be encountered by the beginner in both instrumental and voice training. By the same token, I have omitted many words that are rarely, if ever, encountered by the neophyte.

As in any strange tongue, the language of music can be a complex and frequently baffling form of communication. It consists of unfamiliar signs and strange words whose origins are Latin, Italian, French or German. And yet, usage of this language is as precise for the musician as the equally strange nomenclature of science is for the physicist and chemist. No musician—beginner or advanced—can hope to perform well unless he understands these signs, guides and directions which every composer must employ to indicate how his music is to be played and interpreted.

I have tried to be simple in my definitions while retaining the essential meaning of each term. Where appropriate, some of the history and lore of music have been woven into the text. Paul Hoffmaster's illustrations have been carefully placed to supplement and strengthen the definitions where this is appropriate.

Preface

As the title states, this is an *introduction* to the language of music. Students looking for more exhaustive definitions than are found here should seek them out in the encyclopedic dictionaries to be found in any good public library.

If this book stimulates the beginning student to a greater love and understanding of music, and opens up for him some of the exciting vistas that music offers, then I feel my task will have been worth while.

I cannot close without a word of grateful acknowledgment to the several individuals—outstanding musicians and musicologists in their own right—who read the manuscript and whose comments were indispensable in assuring the maximum clarity and accuracy of the definitions. They include Sidney Forrest of the Peabody Institute of Music; Professor Bryce Jordan of the University of Maryland's Music Department; and Mrs. Rae Korson of the Library of Congress Music Division.

STEPHANIE BARACH

Chevy Chase, Maryland
February, 1962

A GUIDE TO PHONETIC PRONUNCIATIONS USED IN THIS BOOK

a as in far	ah
a as in hand	a
a as in lay	ay
a as in law	aw
e as in the	e
e as in leaf	ee
i as in it	i
i as in police	ee
o as in go	oe
o as in to	oo
o as in top	o
o as in cow	ow
u as in use	yoo
u as in hut	u
au as in applaud	aw
ou as in loud	ow

Syllables in CAPITAL letters are accented: for example, the pronunciation for operetta is given as ah-per-ET-tah.

An Introduction to the Language of Music

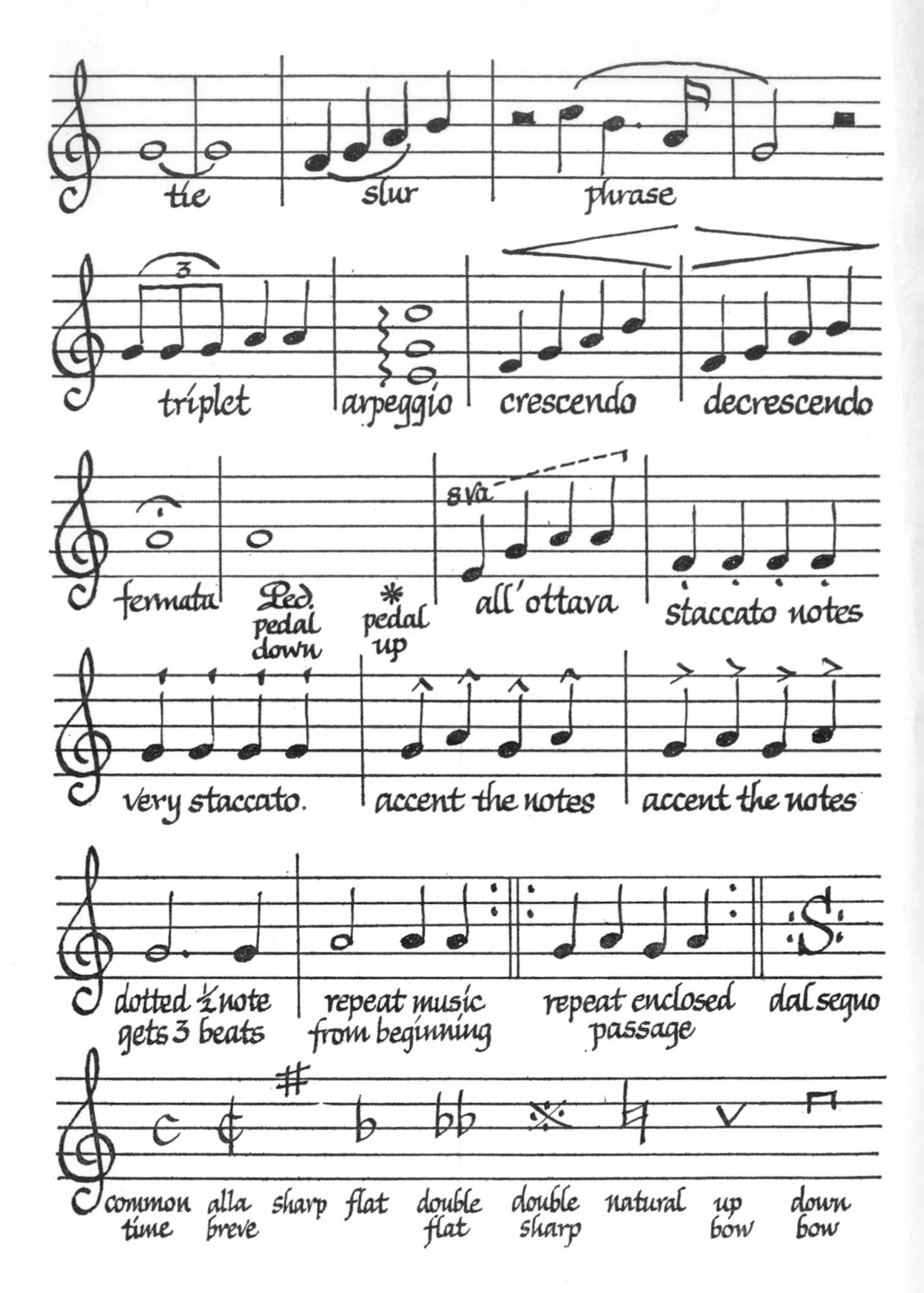
tie
slur
phrase
triplet
arpeggio
crescendo
decrescendo
8va
fermata
Ped.
pedal down
*
pedal up
all'ottava
staccato notes
very staccato.
accent the notes
accent the notes
dotted ½ note gets 3 beats
repeat music from beginning
repeat enclosed passage
dal segno
common time
alla breve
sharp
flat
double flat
double sharp
natural
up bow
down bow

A

A. The sixth note of the C scale. Before an orchestra begins to play, the oboe sounds its *A*. The other instruments are then tuned to that pitch so as to be in tune with one another. Sometimes capital *A* is used to indicate an *A*-major scale or triad. Small *a* represents a minor scale or triad.

a ballata (ah bah-LAH-tah, Italian). Written as a ballad or as a musical story.

a battuta (ah bah-TOO-tah, Italian, "at the beat"). Return to exact time.

Abendmusik (AH-bend-moo-zeek, German). Evening music. Originally, sacred music played in the late afternoon.

absolute pitch. The ability to hear an isolated musical sound and identify its pitch. A person with this ability can sing any specific tone at the correct pitch without the help of an instrument.

a cappella (ah kah-PEL-lah, Italian). At one time meant "in the church style," but now describes music sung by a group of voices without accompaniment.

A CAPPELLA

a capriccio (ah kah-PREE-chee-o, Italian). Play at the fancy of the performer—generally in a light, airy way.

accelerando (ah-chel-er-AN-doe, Italian). Gradually play faster. (*abbrev.* accel.)

accent (AK-sent). The pulse or emphasis which makes one note

of a measure sound more important than the others.

acciaccatura. See appoggiatura.

accidental. A symbol such as a sharp, flat, and natural used to raise or lower the sound of a note. There are five kinds of *accidentals:* 1. A sharp (♯) is a symbol which indicates that the tone goes up a half step. 2. A double sharp (※) is a symbol which indicates that the tone goes up two half steps. 3. A flat (♭) is a symbol which indicates that the tone goes down a half step. 4. A double flat (♭♭) is a symbol which indicates that the tone goes down two half steps. 5. A natural (♮) cancels a sharp or a flat. (Illus. p. xvi)

accompaniment. Music played by an instrument or an orchestra as background music for a solo performance. It makes the total performance sound richer and more complete.

accompanist. A performer who plays a musical background for another musician playing or singing the main part.

accopiato (ah-cop-i-AH-toe, Italian). Couple or tie the notes. In organ playing, pedal two notes to give them a more connected and smoother sound.

accordion. A musical instrument often used by strolling musicians. It has a small piano-type keyboard with about forty-one keys, and buttons which produce bass notes and chords when pressed. The body of the instrument is a folding bellows. Inside are metal reeds which produce sounds as the bellows are squeezed in and pulled out.

ACCORDION

accordionist. Someone who plays the accordion.

acoustics (a-KOOS-tics). The science of sound. It deals with the way sounds are made, transmitted, modified, and heard. The science of *acoustics* is important for the engineer or architect designing a room or hall where music is to be played or where speeches are to be made. For example, in a room with bare walls, one hears many sounds very clearly, but heavy draperies and rugs will muffle the sounds.

action. 1. The way parts of an instrument move to help make the music. Piano *action,* for example is the way in which the hammers strike the strings. 2. The way a

musician uses his fingers, feet, or his voice when he plays or sings or dances.

adagio (ah-DAH-jeeo, Italian). 1. Play or sing slowly. 2. Sometimes, the name given to a slow movement of a sonata or a symphony.

adagio assai (ah-DAH-jeeo ah-SIGH, Italian). Play or sing very slowly.

adagio molto (ah-DAH-jeeo MOLE-toe, Italian). Play or sing more slowly than *adagio assai*.

adapted. Describes music that has been changed or rearranged. For example, music originally written for an entire orchestra may be rewritten, or *adapted,* for the piano. Similarly, music written for the voice may be *adapted* for the violin.

à deux (ah doo, French). For two, as two people playing or singing together.

à deux mains (ah doo man, French). For two hands.

ad libitum (ahd LIB-i-toom, Latin). 1. The player is free to change the time of the music. 2. Also may indicate that a band or orchestra may leave out part of an ensemble.

aeolian harp (ee-OH-lee-an, from Aeolus, the god of the winds, Greek). A long, stringed box hung in a tree or a window which permits the wind to vibrate its strings. Mysterious and strange sounds result. This device was very popular around 1800.

À DEUX

AEOLIAN HARP

aeolian piano (ee-OH-lee-an). A player piano in which music is made by the action of a stream of air passing through tiny holes in a role of paper. *See* **pianola.**

afterbeat. The "and" that you feel and say after you count the regular beat. Example: "One *and* two *and* three *and* . . ." In other words, a pause after each beat.

agitato (ah-ji-TAH-toe, Italian). Play excitedly, with extra energy.

agréments (AH-gray-man, French). Extra notes and trills added to music written for the harpsichord and spinet. Also found in music written for stringed and wind instruments.

air (also **ayre**). Most commonly a melody or a song. In the 16th century, an *air* was a melody written for voice and accompanied by other voices or instruments. By the 17th century *airs* were often written for the lute. Eighteenth-century composers frequently called the slow, melodic movements of their dance suites *airs*.

Albumblatt (AHL-boom-blaht). The German word for "album leaf." Edvard Grieg and other 19th-century composers used this title for a short and simple piece.

al fine (ahl FEE-nay, Italian). Go back and play the piece over to the *fine*, or end. *See* ***da capo al fine*** and ***dal segno al fine.***

alla breve (ah-lah BRAY-vay, Italian). A tempo mark (₵) meaning quick duple time. The half note is the basic unit of time and the meter signature is 2/2. (Illus. p. xvi)

alla marcia (ah-lah MAR-chia, Italian). Play or sing like a march.

all' ottava (ahl oh-TAHV-ah, Italian). Passages in a score marked *all' 8va* (or simply *8va*) are to be played an octave higher or lower. If the *8va* sign is printed above the notes, the passage is to be raised an octave. If below, the passage is to be lowered. (*abbrev.* ott. or 8va) (Illus. p. xvi)

allargando (ahl-lar-GAN-doe, Italian). Gradually let the sound grow louder and the tempo get slower at the same time. (*abbrev.* allarg.)

allegretto (ahl-le-GRET-toe, Italian). Play in a lively, quick manner. (*abbrev.* allgtto.)

allegro (ahl-LEG-groe, Italian). Play fast, briskly, like a march. (*abbrev.* all.)

allegro brilliante (ahl-LEG-groe bril-YAHN-tay, Italian). Play quickly or briskly with boldness, as if you want to show off what you can do.

allegro molto (ahl-LEG-groe MOLE-toe, Italian). Allegro with a push!

allegro non tanto (ah-LEG-groe non TAHN-toe, Italian). Play quickly or briskly, but don't overdo it.

allemande (ahl-le-MOND, French). A German dance in 2/4 or 2/2 time. Sometimes moderately slow, sometimes lively. Also can be a dance movement in a suite.

alto (AL-toe, Italian, "high"). The range in music in the treble staff written for low-pitched voices which reach from F below middle C to the D above middle C. An *alto* part is usually sung by women and young boys. The viola is sometimes called the *alto* of the string family.

alto clef. A clef which indicates that the third line of the staff is to be read as middle C. Also known as the "viola clef." *See* **clef.**

amateur. As applied to music, someone who plays, sings, or dances for his own pleasure, not for his living.

andante (ahn-DAHN-tay, Italian, "going" or "walking"). Play rather slowly.

andantino (ahn-dahn-TEEN-o, Italian). Slowly, but with a slight urgency to quicken.

Anfang (AHN-fang, German). Beginning.

animato (ahn-i-MAH-toe, Italian). Play or sing with pep and spirit. (*abbrev.* anim.)

anthem. A choral composition, usually accompanied by an organ, sung at Protestant church services. The words of the composition are English translations of the Bible or other religious texts. A *national anthem* is the official patriotic song of a country.

antiphonal music. Music in which one group of performers answers another. For example, two choirs alternating in a song are singing *antiphonal music.* Similarly, the words describe music in which one section of an orchestra gives way to another section.

aperto (ah-PEAR-toe, Italian). Use open or full sound. On the piano, this sound is created by use of the damper or right pedal.

a poco (ah POKE-oh, Italian). Little by little, or gradually.

appassionata (ah-pas-seeo-NAH-tah, Italian). Play with great feeling. One of Beethoven's greatest piano works was the *Sonata appassionata.*

appoggiatura (ah-poj-ee-ah-TOOR-ah, Italian, "to lean upon"). There are two kinds of *appoggiaturas.* The first is the *short appoggiatura* (now sometimes called the "acciaccatura"), a very short grace note played on almost the same beat as the principal note. The grace note does not borrow any special time value from the principal note. The second type, the *long appoggiatura,* has a definite accent when played or sung, and borrows a portion of the time value of the principal note. The *appoggiatura* is frequently used in harpsichord playing.

arabesque (a-ra-BESK). Originally a kind of ornamentation in Arab architecture. Robert Schumann, Claude Debussy and other composers borrowed the word as a name for some of their compositions, perhaps because the music reminded them of the beautiful Arab decorations.

arco (AHR-koe, Italian). 1. Bow for a stringed instrument. 2. Begin using the bow again after a pizzicato (or string-plucking) passage.

arco saltando (AHR-koe sal-TAHN-doe, Italian). Let the bow bounce so quickly on the string that it will rebound. The result is a sound like a quick staccato.

aria (AH-ree-a, Italian). A song or melody in a cantata, an oratorio or an opera which gives the singer an opportunity to display vocal ability. An *aria* is sung by one person, with an accompaniment.

arioso (ah-ree-OH-so, Italian). A type of solo writing for the voice, used in operas, oratorios, and cantatas. It is partly like an aria, partly like a recitative in style.

arpeggio (ar-PEJ-ee-o, Italian). The notes of a chord played one after another, beginning either at the bottom and going up, or at the top and going down. (*abbrev.* arp.) (Illus. p. xvi)

arrangement. A musical piece rewritten from the original so that it can be performed by different instruments.

arranger. A musician who rewrites or adapts music so that it can be played or sung in many different ways. An *arranger* may rewrite a piano piece so that it can be played by an orchestra, or a popular song may be arranged for a dance band.

art songs. Songs usually composed for concert performance by trained composers. Franz Schubert was a genius of the *art song.* He developed and created the lied (German, meaning "song"), in which the words and the music were woven together in a new, dramatic way. By the 19th century, the piano accompaniment to an *art song* was used almost independently to build up the mood and heighten the drama of the song.

a tempo (ah TEM-po, Italian). Return to the original tempo.

atonality (ay-tone-AL-ity). A system of 20th-century composition in which no key is used. Usually, *atonality* makes use of the twelve-tone scale. Arnold Schönberg used this system in his *Three Piano Pieces.*

attack. The beginning of the production of a particular tone. Thus, we can say to a pianist, "Use a stronger *attack* on the B."

augmented. Made larger. An *augmented* interval is one half step larger than a major interval. *See* **interval.** (*abbrev.* aug.)

B

Bachelor of Music. The degree usually given college students who complete four years of study of music. (*abbrev.* Mus.B.)

background music. Music played as part of a movie, radio program, or television show to make the story more real, dramatic, or enjoyable.

bagatelle. A "trifle" or short piece, written for piano or other instruments. Beethoven wrote three sets of *bagatelles* for the piano.

bagpipe. A very old wind instrument with a bag to which reed pipes are attached. The player fills the bag with air either by blowing into it through a mouthpiece or by pumping a bellows which he carries under his arm. The air is forced out of the bag through the set of pipes, which produces a very shrill sound. The instrument was originally introduced into Europe by the Romans in the 1st century. Today *bagpipes* are usually associated with Scotland.

BAGPIPE

balalaika (bah-lah-LIKE-ah, Russian). A three-stringed version of the guitar. It is very popular in Russia where it is used as an accompaniment to songs and dances. First used by the Tartars in central Asia in the 13th century.

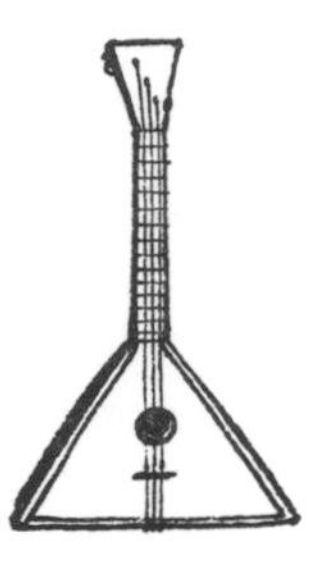

BALALAIKA

ballad (bal-led). 1. Long ago, a song accompanied by dances. 2. Later, a story in prose or verse set to music.

BALLAD (FRANKIE AND JOHNNIE)

ballade (bal-AHD). In the 19th and 20th centuries, a romantic kind of composition. Chopin wrote beautiful *ballades* for the piano.

ballad opera. A type of stage entertainment popular in England in the 18th century, consisting of spoken dialogue and simple songs whose tunes were borrowed from folk songs or from the serious operas of the time. A prime example, *The Beggar's Opera,* was first performed in 1728, and is still frequently heard today either in its original form or in modern versions.

ballata (bal-LAH-tah). A 14th-century Italian song consisting of poetry set to music. *Ballatas* were used as an accompaniment for dancing.

ballerina (bal-ler-REE-na, Italian). A female ballet dancer.

ballet (BAL-lay, French). A dance play, set to orchestral music, that tells a story. The dancers' costumes and the colorful scenery help to make the performance dramatic. *Ballets* were an important part of French and Italian court entertainment during the Renaissance. They are still tremendously popular all over the world.

balleto (bal-LET-toe, Italian). Italian word for ballet.

band. A group of musicians playing woodwind, brass and percussion instruments. Members of the *band* tune to the B♭ pitch to be in tune with one another.

bandmaster. Conductor or leader of the band.

banjo (from the word *bandore,* meaning "guitar," which slaves pronounced "banjo"). A round four- or five-stringed instrument, shaped like a drum, with a long, straight neck. The strings are plucked by the fingers directly, or with the aid of a pick. The *banjo* was brought to America by Negro slaves from Africa.

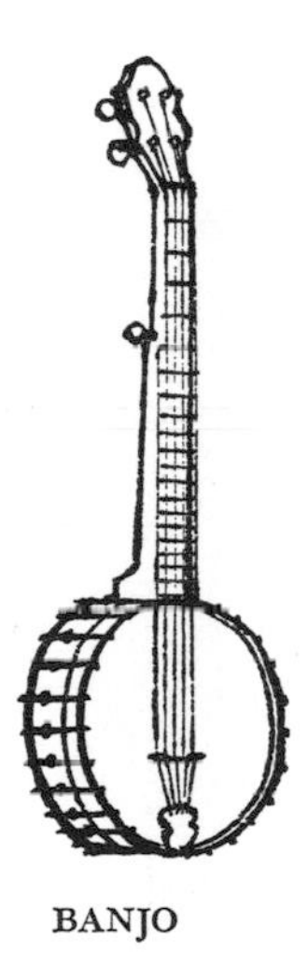

BANJO

bar. 1. The line drawn through a musical staff to mark off the measures. 2. **double bar.** A double line indicating the end of the music.

barcarole (BAHR-ca-rolle, from the Italian *barca,* "boat"). A quiet song whose rhythm imitates the gentle rocking of a boat. *Barcaroles* were originally sung by Venetian gondoliers as they guided their boats through the canals of Venice.

baritone. A man's medium-low singing voice which falls between bass and tenor, with a range from the second G below middle C to the first E above middle C.

barn dance. An American folk-dance party, originally held to celebrate the completion of a new barn built by a farmer with the aid of his neighbors. "Paul Jones" is a popular dance performed at such celebrations.

baroque music. Music composed in the 150-year period from 1600 to 1750 during which musical composition became more elaborate and dramatic. This period brought tremendous strides in the development of instrumental and vocal forms.

barré (bar-RAY, French). In guitar playing: put the forefinger of the left hand across the strings to stop the sound.

bass (base). The lowest male singing voice. Its range is from the low E on the *bass* staff to middle C.

bass clarinet. A single-reed woodwind instrument, about 34 inches long, pitched in B♭ with a range an octave lower than the ordinary clarinet.

BASS CLARINET

bass clef. A sign which indicates that the fourth line of a staff is to be read as F. Music for the notes below middle C is generally written on a staff containing a *bass clef* sign. It is sometimes called the F clef. *See* **clef** for illustration.

bass drum. A large round percussion instrument of unfixed pitch. It consists of a cylindrical frame covered with tightly stretched pieces of calfskin. The player strikes the calfskin with a felt-headed stick, producing a deep booming sound.

BASS DRUM

basso obbligato (BAHS-so ob-li-GAH-toe, Italian). A bass part necessary to the music being played.

BASSOON

bassoon (bas-SOON). A reddish-brown woodwind instrument with a deep voice, used in orchestras and bands. It has a double reed and ranges slightly over three octaves. Most of the *bassoon's* music is written in the bass clef. The instrument is the bass member of the oboe family.

bassoonist (bas-SOON-ist). A bassoon player.

baton (bah-TAHN). The stick a conductor uses to lead the orchestra. By watching the *baton* the musicians are able to follow the conductor and play together in exact time. Conductors began to use the *baton* in 1820.

BATON

beat. The pulse of the music. The duration of a *beat* depends upon the time signature and the speed of the movement.

bebop (also **bop**). A type of jazz developed in the early 1940's characterized by a fast tempo and much dissonance. Dizzy Gillespie and Charlie Parker are two of the best known *bebop* artists.

bel canto (bel CAHN-toe, Italian, "beautiful song"). A style of singing which became popular in Italy in the 18th century when teachers taught singers to use the voice in a smoother, more beautiful, and fuller way.

bellows. In music, a device for driving a strong current of air through the pipes or reeds of an organ or through the valves of an accordion.

bene (BEN-eh, Italian). Well. For example *bene tenuto* means "hold the note well."

bene tenuto (BEN-ay ten-OO-toe, Italian). Hold the note well and surely.

ben marcato (ben mar-CAH-toe, Italian). Use a strong, clear accent.

berceuse (bear-SOOZE, French). A cradle song or lullaby.

binary form. A musical form in which a composition is divided into two sections known as "A" and "B." Each section is usually repeated when played or sung. The form was popular during the classical period in the 18th and 19th centuries, and is often found in romantic 19th-century piano compositions.

blues. A twelve-bar vocal and instrumental jazz piece in which the third and seventh tones are flatted to give the melody a sad, complaining quality. Originally a spiritual or sorrowful post-Civil War slave song sung in the fields. Now, a type of song that complains about man's earthly troubles. The first published *blues* song was "The Memphis Blues," written in 1912 by W. C. Handy. Handy's most famous and remembered work is "The St. Louis Blues."

bolero (bo-LAIR-oh, Spanish). A lively Spanish dance in 3/4 time accompanied by clicking castanets and sometimes gay, excited singing. Danced as a solo or with a partner. Ravel wrote a famous *bolero* for orchestra.

bones. Two pieces of wood clicked together in the hand like castanets. Probably first used in the 16th century. Gradually became popular in minstrel shows.

bongo drum. A drum open on one end and covered by a calfskin

BONGO DRUMS

head on the other. *Bongo drums* were originally used by Africans, who made them from hollow tree trunks of varying lengths covered at one end with stretched animal skins. Later they appeared in the islands of the Caribbean. Today, they are used in jazz and Latin-American bands as rhythmic accompaniment. The player usually holds the drums between his knees and beats out the rhythm with his hands and fingers.

boogie-woogie. A type of jazz piano music in which the left hand hits a steady 8/8 rhythm, usually playing a series of broken octaves which move in scalelike patterns, while the right hand plays a melody. *Boogie-woogie* music is also sometimes arranged for dance bands. It was the forerunner of rock-and-roll music.

bop. See **bebop.**

bourrée (boor-RAY, French). A quick, happy 17th-century dance in 2/4 time, of French and Spanish origin.

bow. A long, narrow piece of wood to which is attached finely drawn horsehair. The device is used in

BOW

playing stringed instruments such as the violin, viola, cello, and double bass. A rectangular nut holds the hair together at the bottom of the *bow* and controls the tension. The *bow* causes the strings to vibrate when drawn across them, creating tones. A Frenchman, François Tourte, perfected the *bow* at the end of the 18th century.

bow hand. The hand that holds the bow.

bow instruments. The four stringed instruments (violin, viola, cello, double bass) played with a bow.

bowing. Using the bow according to the tempo marks which tell the player to play fast or slow, loud or soft, or to bow up or down.

BRASS BAND

brace. The curved line at the left of the staff that seems to hold it together.

brass band. A band made up of brass instruments: trumpets, tubas, French horns, trombones, and the like.

brass choir. An instrumental group made up of trumpets, French horns, trombones, tubas, and cornets.

brass instruments. *See* **instruments.**

break. 1. In singing, the point at which the high notes, or head register, change to the low notes or chest register. 2. In a clarinet, the change from B-flat to B natural in the staff above middle C. 3. In jazz music, the moment when a member of the band (such as the pianist or a horn player) improvises his own variations on the melody.

breathing marks. The signs that tell a singer when to take a breath to start a new phrase.

bridge. 1. The upright piece on the belly of a stringed instrument over which the strings cross to reach the pegs. 2. A line or bar connecting notes.

brioso (bree-OH-soe, Italian). Play in a lively, vigorous way.

broken chord. An arpeggio. A chord whose notes are played one after another, not all at once.

buffo (BOOF-oe, Italian). The funny man in an opera. A clown, a music comedian.

BUFFO

BUGLE

bugle. A brass or copper instrument used for military purposes and by scouts and campers. Sounds "taps," "reveille" and similar calls. The *bugle* has no valves; all pitch changes are made by lipping.

C

cadence (from Latin *cadens,* "to fall"). Two or more chords that seem to "fall" at the end of a phrase, section, or tune.

cadenza (ka-DEN-za, Italian). The music near the end of a movement of a concerto or near the end of an aria, usually written to give the performer a chance to show his virtuosity in playing or singing. In the 18th century *cadenzas* were usually improvised. Mozart wrote out some of his. Brahms was one of the last composers to use improvised *cadenzas.* (*abbrev.* cad.)

cakewalk. Originally, a gay Negro dance around a cake set in the middle of a table. The person who, at a given signal first touched the cake, won it. The dance was in any step, from a strut to a simple bouncing walk. Debussy wrote a famous *cakewalk* song, "The Golliwogs' Cakewalk."

CAKEWALK

calando (ka-LAN-do, Italian). Gradually play or sing slower and more quietly. (*abbrev.* cal.)

camp meeting songs. Usually religious hymns and songs sung at outdoor religious meetings and revivals.

canon. A piece of choral music in which two or more voices play follow-the-leader. The lead voice starts a tune, and all the other voices must follow exactly the same way. When a *canon* returns to the beginning of the tune without a break, it is called a round. The earliest *canon* we know of is "Sumer is Icumen In," written about 1310.

cantabile (kahn-TAH-bill-lay, Italian). Make the music sing.

cantata (kahn-TAH-ta, Italian). A composition for voices and instruments which usually consists of a number of movements such as choruses, arias, recitatives, duets, and chorales. *Cantatas* were very popular in 17- and 18th-century Italy where they were generally written on nonreligious subjects and sung by solo voices. German composers of the same period were better known for the religious *cantatas* which they wrote for the Lutheran church services. Johann Sebastian Bach wrote about 200 religious *cantatas* and is considered to be master of the form. *Cantatas* have been written by many leading 20th-century composers.

cantor (KAN-tor). A singer in religious services (usually in a Jewish synagogue) who performs solo chants. In the German Protestant church a *cantor* is a director of music.

capo (KAH-poe, Italian, "head"). The beginning of a piece of music. *See da capo al fine.*

capriccio (kah-PREE-chee-oe, Italian). A short, light or lively piano piece.

carillon (KAR-ee-yon, French). Groups of bells, usually mounted in a tower. They are connected with a keyboard, and sounded by striking the keys. First used in Holland, Luxembourg, and Belgium around 1500.

carol. A happy song usually sung at Christmastime. Developed from the religious folk songs or dancing songs of the 15th century. The oldest printed *carol,* an English one called "The Boar's Head," dates from around 1521. *Carols* have been handed down from generation to generation.

castanets (kas-ta-NETS). Two wooden shells tied together, held

CASTANETS

in the hand, and rhythmically clapped in time with the music. *Castanets* are used in many Spanish dances to accent the movement of the dance. They are also used as a percussion instrument in the symphony orchestra.

C clef. A sign to show the staff position of middle C on the alto, tenor, soprano, and mezzo-soprano clefs. The *C clef* is movable. In more advanced music, both the treble and bass clefs are also movable. *See* **clef.**

celesta (se-LES-ta, Italian). A percussion instrument, resembling a small piano, containing a four-octave keyboard ranging upward from middle C. Playing on the keyboard sets in motion a set of hammers, which in turn strike a set of metal bars, producing a clear, bell-like tone. The *celesta* was invented by Auguste Mustel in 1886.

cellist (CHEL-list, Italian). Abbreviation for violoncellist. A cello player.

cello (CHEL-loe, Italian). Abbreviation for violoncello. A member of the violin family, with a mellow, low, expressive tone. The *cello* is held between the knees when played. It has four strings tuned to C, G, D, A, and is an octave lower in sound than the viola. The *cello* uses the bass clef. There are eight to twelve *celli* in a full symphony orchestra. (Illus. p. 112)

chaconne (sha-KON, French). 1. A slow, stately, graceful Spanish dance in 3/4 time. Originally came from Mexico to Spain at the end of the 16th century. 2. A set of variations based on a short theme. Bach wrote a famous *chaconne* for the violin.

chamber music. Music especially written to be played in a small hall or room. Usually string quartets, trios, or small combinations of players perform this type of music. In *chamber music,* one part is written for each performer, while in orchestral music, one part may be written for several performers who play the same kind of instrument.

chamber orchestra. A modern term meaning a small orchestra made up of a string and woodwind group. Sometimes a trumpet and one or two French horns are added. Usually there are twenty-five to thirty players.

chant. A religious song without accompaniment and without strict time. A good example is Gregorian chant, also called plainsong, which consists of Roman Catholic church texts set to music. The earliest *chants* go back to Greek, Hindu, Arabic, and Hebrew ritual services.

chest tone. A tone sung in the lower registers of the voice.

chimes. A percussion instrument used in a symphony orchestra, and consisting of about eighteen bells hung from a frame. The bells are tuned to a scale and sound is produced by striking them with wooden mallets.

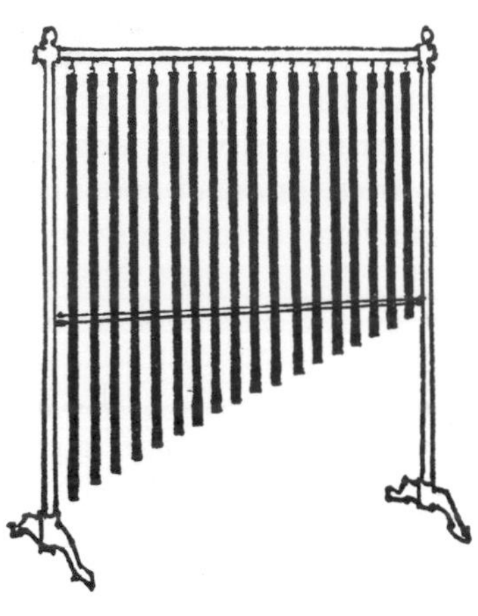

CHIMES

choir. 1. A group of singers usually assembled to perform in a church. A *full choir* has soprano, alto, tenor, and bass members. 2. A group of instrument voices that play together. In the orchestra, the *string choir* includes the violin, viola, cello, and double bass. There are also *woodwind, brass,* and *percussion choirs* in the orchestra.

choir master. The leader or conductor of a choir.

choral music (KOR-el). Music sung by a chorus or choir.

chorale (ko-RAL). Protestant prayers or hymns set to music. Introduced into German church services by Martin Luther in the 16th century to provide music for the congregation. Cantatas are often based on *chorales.*

chord (KORD). A combination of tones sounded together.

choreographer (kor-ee-OG-ra-fer). One who creates dances or ballets and shows how they are to be performed before an audience. A *choreographer* is to his dance what a composer is to his music.

chorus. 1. A group of singers. 2. The catchy, melodic part of many popular songs; a refrain.

chromatic. A description of music containing many of the half-step intervals not found in a diatonic scale.

chromatic keys. The black and white keys of the piano in half-step sequence.

chromatic scale. A scale of twelve notes in which all of the intervals are half steps.

clarinet (from the French, "little bell"). A woodwind instrument consisting of a cylindrical body, made of metal or wood, with a single-reed mouthpiece at one end and a bell-shaped opening at the other. To play it, the clarinetist blows a stream of air through the mouthpiece while fingering a set of keys and holes. *Clarinets* are pitched in many keys, most commonly B♭, and have a range of more than three octaves. There

CLARINET

are usually four *clarinet* players in a full symphony orchestra. In a band, where as many as thirty *clarinets* are used, the instrument is as important as a violin is to an orchestra.

clarinetist. A clarinet player.

classical music. Music written by the classical composers according to their rules of form and harmony. *See* **classical school.**

classical school. A group of composers who lived in the period from 1750 to 1825. While striving for beauty in melody, they placed high value on balance and austerity in form. The most famous composers of the classical group were Mozart, Haydn, Beethoven, and Schubert. Many musicians feel that their work was so outstanding that its quality has never been surpassed.

clavichord. A keyboard instrument, an ancestor of the piano, which originated around the 13th century. Its strings are not hit by hammers, but by upright metal wedges called "tangents." The sound of the *clavichord* is weaker than the piano's, but very expressive.

CLAVICHORD

clef. A sign placed at the beginning of the staff which indicates the sound range of the music. 1. The *treble* or *G clef* is so named because it indicates that the second line of the staff is to be read as G. 2. The *bass* or *F clef* is placed on the fourth line of the staff and indicates that this line is to be read as F. 3. The *C clef* can be moved up or down the staff, but the center of the *C clef* is always middle C. If its center is on the fourth line, it is called a *tenor clef;* on the third line, *alto clef;* on the first line, *soprano clef*.

CLEFS

close harmony. Harmony in which the three upper voice parts fall within one octave of one another.

coda (KO-dah, Italian, "tail"). A tune added after the main song is finished, like a postscript in a letter. Also, an ending to a movement in sonata form. *See* **sonata form.**

col legno (KOL LEYN-yo, Italian, "with the wood"). Tap the strings of a violin with the wooden part of the bow.

coloratura (kol-or-ah-TUR-ah, Italian, "colored"). 1. Elaborate, decorated, rapid passages of a vocal melody. Trills, roulades, and cadenzas are features of *coloratura* passages, which are often found in 18th- and 19th-century Italian operas. 2. **coloratura soprano.** A high-pitched voice capable of meeting the demands of difficult *coloratura* passages.

combo. In jazz language, a slang word for "combination." A *combo* is a small band usually consisting of three to eight members. A three-man *combo* usually includes a piano, string bass, and drums.

common time. 4/4 time. Indicated by the sign "C." (Illus. p. xvi)

composer. A persons who writes original music.

composition. Original music created by a composer.

con (Italian, "with"). For example, *con brio* means "with vigor."

con agilita (con ah-JEEL-ee-tah, Italian). Play or sing very quickly or easily, with agility.

con brio (con BREE-oh, Italian). Play or sing with vigor and power.

concert (KON-sert). Literally, and in the older sense, a "playing together." Now, more usually, a public musical performance. By the 18th century, people began to pay admission to hear music performed in public.

concert grand. The biggest grand piano, 10 feet from front to back. Used mostly in concert halls.

concert master. The leader of the first violinists in an orchestra. He sits nearest to the conductor and occasionally acts as his assistant or substitutes for him.

concerto (kon-CHAIR-toe, Italian). A musical composition usually in three movements played by a single instrument (piano or violin, for example) accompanied by a large orchestra. In a *double concerto* two instruments are the soloists. The *concerto* theme is the major melody of the piece played separately or together by the soloist and orchestra.

Conzertstück (CON-zert-shtick, German). A concert piece, similar to a short concerto, for one or more solo instruments with orchestra.

conductor. The director or leader of an orchestra. By beating time

CONDUCTOR

with a baton, moving his hands and body and face expressively, he interprets the music and directs the players. He gives them their entrance cues. He fixes the correct tempo; he imparts the proper feeling or mood. The players observe and obey his gestures and directions, and thus together play like a single musical family, that is, an orchestra.

conservatory. In music, a school which teaches such subjects as instrument playing, voice training, theory, harmony, composition, conducting, and music history. The first *conservatories* were started in Italy in the 16th century.

consonant. Describing tones which when sounded at the same time produce an effect pleasing to the ear.

con sordino (con sor-DEE-noe, Italian). Mute or soften the sound of a trumpet or stringed instrument. Various devices can be used for muting. For example, a conical plug is put into the flaring end of brass instruments. Sometimes, a player uses his hand to muffle the French horn. On the piano, the soft pedal is used as a mute.

contra bassoon. A bass woodwind instrument, which sounds the lowest notes in an orchestra. It can growl and make low gruff sounds. The tube of the *contra bassoon* is 16 feet long, but is bent back on itself so that the player can hold and use it. A full symphony orchestra contains one *contra bassoon.* The instrument is played by one of the regular bassoonists.

CONTRA BASSOON

contralto (kon-TRAL-toe, Italian). Another name for the alto, or lower-pitched female voice with a range of two octaves in the treble staff, from a low F below middle C to a high G on the fifth space.

contrapuntal. Having to do with counterpoint.

contrary motion. Two melodic lines or groups of sounds moving in opposite directions at the same time.

cornet. A brass wind instrument, first used in the 19th century, with three valves and pitched in B♭. (It is convertible to A by a valve mechanism or slide.) The *cornet* is shorter than the trumpet and is easier to play. Its wider

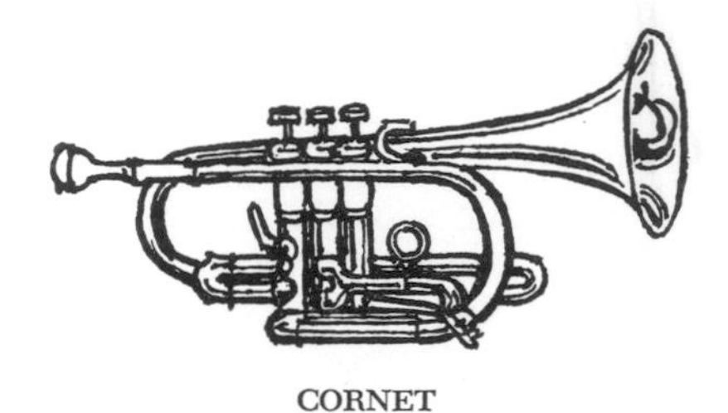

CORNET

bore makes it more flexible. Used in both brass and military bands, it also finds a place in the orchestra. Music for the *cornet* is written in the treble clef. Its range is from F♯ below middle C to the C two lines above the staff.

corps de ballet (KOR de bal-LAY, French). The main group of dancers in a ballet, but not including the leading dancers or soloists.

cotillion. A lively dance, popular in England and the United States in the 19th century, characterized by fancy square-dancelike figures with variations. There was a continual change of partners with the dancers imitating the leading couple. Danced to polkas, mazurkas, and waltzes. Today a *cotillion* is a fancy dress-up ball.

count. Keep exact time in music.

counterpoint. Combining melodies

so that they sound as if they belong together. In a contrapuntal work, though the melodies are mixed, each retains its identity; it is the mixture and offsetting of the melodies and rhythms, one against the other, that produces the harmonic fabric of the entire composition.

courante (koo-RAHNT). The old French dance in 3/4 or 3/8 time performed in the late 16th and 17th centuries. *Courante* means "to run." Thus it is performed very fast. Bach used the *courante* form often as part of his suites for the harpsichord and the clavichord in the early 18th century.

countertenor. *See* **tenor.**

cowboy songs. American folk songs sung by cowboys on the range expressing their loneliness or love for the out-of-doors. First sung in the early 19th century as the pioneers migrated to the West. "Red River Valley" and "Home on the Range" are two favorites.

COWBOY SONGS

CORPS DE BALLET

crescendo (kre-SHEN-doe, Italian). Make the music gradually grow louder. (*abbrev.* cres., cresc.) (Illus. p. xvi)

csardas (CHAHR-dush, Hungarian). A Hungarian dance made up of two parts: a slow part called "lassu" and a gay lively part called "friss" or quickstep. Franz Liszt used the *csardas* in his Hungarian rhapsodies.

CSARDAS

cue. The signal given a musician in an orchestra telling him it is his turn to play. The conductor gives the *cue,* but the player has been warned by the notations on his music to be ready to enter on the proper beat. The notations comprise the concluding notes of parts being played by other members of the orchestra, immediately preceding the *cue* for the entering player.

cymbals. A percussion instrument made up of pairs of circular metal plates, usually brass, about 12 inches in diameter. The *cymbals,* which are held in the hand, are sounded by clashing them together. The range of sound is wide, from very soft to very loud. Smaller *cymbals* resembling castanets were used to provide the tempo in ancient dancing.

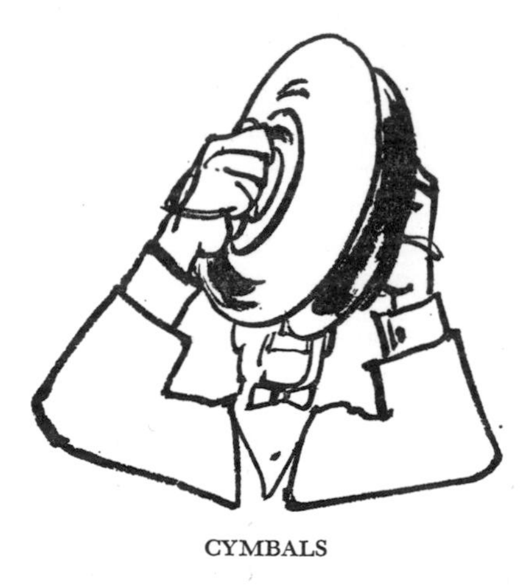

CYMBALS

D

da capo (da KAH-poe, Italian, *capo* "head"). Return to the head or beginning of the piece.

da capo al fine (da KAH-poe al FEE-nay, Italian). Return to the beginning of the piece, and play to the word *fine,* which means "finish." (*abbrev.* D.C.)

dal segno (dahl SEN-yoe, Italian). Return to the sign :S: (*abbrev.* dals s., d.s.) (Illus. p. xvi)

dal segno al fine (dahl SEN-yoe al FEE-nay, Italian). Play from the sign :S: to the end.

damper pedal. The piano pedal most often used. It is on the right-hand side under the instrument. When the *damper pedal* is pushed down with the right foot, the dampers are pulled away from the strings, which permits them to continue vibrating and producing sounds. When the foot is removed from the pedal, the dampers drop back on the strings and the sounds are stopped. The *damper pedal* is sometimes called the "loud pedal."

dampers. Felt-padded blocks of wood that rest on the strings of a piano. *See* **pianoforte.**

dance band. A group of instrumentalists who play primarily for popular dancing. *Dance bands* usually contain three to five saxophone players, some of whom may also play the clarinet or the flute; a brass section consisting of two to four trumpets and one to four trombones; and a rhythm section consisting of piano, drums, string bass, and sometimes a guitar. Occasionally a section of three or four violins is added.

debut (DAY-byoo, French). In music, the first time a musician performs in public.

deciso (day-CHEE-so, Italian). Play more firmly and with push.

decrescendo (de-kre-SHEN-doe, Italian). Gradually get softer in sound. The opposite of crescendo. (*abbrev.* decresc.) (Illus. p. xvi)

degree. 1. One of the tones of a diatonic scale. 2. A line or space of a staff.

dervish dance. A whirling, excited, East Indian dance.

descriptive music (also called program music). Music that illustrates a story or relates to a historical fact. Tschaikowsky's "1812 Overture" written about the war of 1812 is a good example.

détaché (DE-tash-ay, French). Strong, firm, unconnected sounds made by alternate up-and-down bowing.

development. How music grows—from a seed to a full tree. First are the tones, then the motive, phrase, section, movement, and finally the complete, finished piece of music. In other words, *development* is the pronouncement, exploration, and elaboration of a musical idea.

diapason (DIE-a-PAY-son, from the Greek, "through all"). A complete scale or range of sounds. In an organ, the two 8-foot pipes that have the sound of an entire keyboard. (*abbrev.* diap.)

diatonic. A term describing the major and minor scales according to their patterns as opposed to the chromatic scale.

diatonic scale. One of the standard major or minor scales. *See* **major scale, minor scale.**

diminished. Made smaller. A *diminished* interval is one half step smaller than a major interval. *See* **interval.**

diminuendo (di-min-yoo-END-o, Italian). Gradually get softer. Opposite of crescendo. (*abbrev.* dim.)

dissonance. Two or more sounds in conflict or clashing with each other.

diva (DEE-vah, Italian). A woman singer who has the leading role in grand opera. A prima donna.

divertimento (di-vert-i-MEN-toe, Italian). 1. An instrumental composition in several short movements written for a chamber group or orchestra, often used as entertainment in the 18th century. 2. Songs or dances performed between the acts or near the end of an opera.

Dixie Land (also **Dixie**). An early, and now classic, type of jazz which originated in such southern cities as New Orleans, Mobile and Memphis in the first part of this century. *Dixie Land* is characterized by a simple two-beat rhythm and by its use of syncopation. Among the best *Dixie Land* artists have been Sidney Bechet, King Oliver, and Louis Armstrong.

divisi (di-VEE-see, Italian, "divided"). A section of an orchestra (such as the first violins) is to divide and play two or more separate parts.

dolce (DOL-chay, Italian). Play or sing sweetly, gently. (*abbrev.* dol.)

dolcissimo (dol-CHISS-eemoe, Italian). Play or sing very sweetly, very gently. (*abbrev.* dolcis.)

doloroso (dol-or-ROE-soe, Italian). Play or sing very sadly.

dominant. The fifth tone in the major or minor scale.

dominant chord. A chord starting on the fifth note in its major or minor scale.

doppio pedale (DOP-yoe pe-DAHL-lay, Italian). The feet play two notes on the organ pedals at the same time. The notes are usually an octave apart.

dot. 1. A sign placed after a note which means to increase the time duration of the note by half its original value. 2. If above or below the note, it means "make the note jump," or "sound staccato." (Illus. p. xvi)

double bar. A *heavy double bar* drawn through the staff to mark the end of the music. A *light double bar* drawn through the staff marks the end of one movement and the beginning of another. The *light double bar* is also sometimes used to divide sections of one movement.

double bass. The largest member of the violin family. It is so tall (6 feet high) that the player must stand up or sit on a high stool to play it. It has four strings tuned to E, A, D, G. Music for the *double bass* is written on the bass clef to avoid the use of leger lines, but it sounds an octave lower than written. There can be as many as nine *double basses* in a full symphony orchestra. (Illus. p. 112)

double bassoon. *See* **contra bassoon.**

double flat. A sign placed before a note, which means "go down two half steps or one whole step." *See* **accidentals.** (Illus. p. xvi)

double quartet. Music for eight separate voices or instruments performing together.

double reed. Two pieces of cane joined together as a mouthpiece in certain woodwind instruments, such as the oboe, English horn, or bassoon.

double sharp. A sign placed before a note, meaning "go up two half steps, or one whole step." *See* **accidentals.** (Illus. p. xvi)

double stop. Play two or more notes by stopping two or more strings at the same time.

double tongue. A method of playing flute and brass instruments. It consists of moving the tongue very quickly, first against the back of the front teeth, then against the roof of the mouth, which produces a sharp staccato sound.

double whole note (also **double note**). A note held twice as long as a whole note. *See* **notes and rests.**

downbeat. The strong first accented beat in a measure.

down bow. Draw the entire length of the bow left to right, across the strings, from bottom to the top. An instruction sign for violin, viola, cello, and double-bass players. (Illus. p. xvi)

doxology. A religious song in praise of God.

drone. The low, moaning, persistent tones of a bagpipe, played against the melody of the song. *Drone* sounds are usually a parallel fifth or octave apart.

drum. A percussion instrument made of a round wooden or metal frame which is covered, top and bottom, by a stretched dried animal skin. Orchestras usually have three types of *drums: snare drum, bass drum,* and *kettle drums,* which are also called "tympani."

drum major. The leader of a group of drummers or of a band. He leads the drummers and band when they march.

drummer. A musician who plays the drums.

duet. Music sung, played, or danced by two persons.

dulcimer. A very old triangular-shaped stringed instrument consisting of wires stretched over a sound box which are struck with

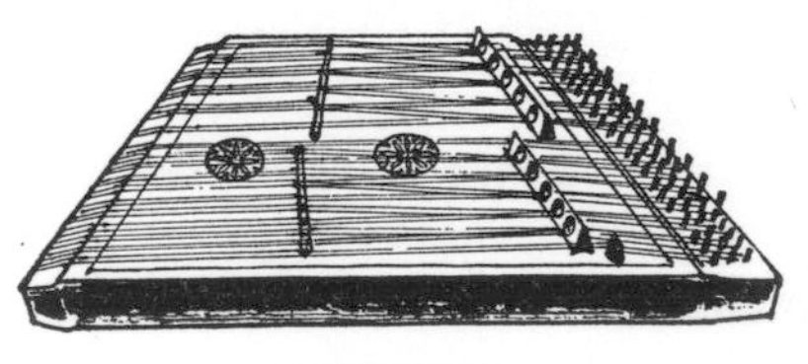

DULCIMER

hammers to produce sound. The *dulcimer* has a range of two to three octaves. It originated in the Orient and from there was carried to Western Europe, where the gypsies, who call it the cimbalon, still use it. It is also played to this day in the mountain areas of the United States as accompaniment for songs and hillbilly music.

duo. Same as duet.

duple time (DOO-pul). A rhythm pattern in which there are two (or some multiple of two) beats to a measure, with an accent on the first beat. Examples: 2/2 or 2/4 time.

dynamics. The loudness and softness of music.

E

ear. In music, to have a good *ear* is to have the ability to keep or follow a tune, to detect false notes, to perceive subtleties of harmony, to recognize changes in pitch. To what extent a good *ear* is inherent talent, to what extent training, is not clear, but the expression is intended to describe an innate feeling for melody and a sense of rhythm.

ear training. Training in the ability to distinguish one musical pitch from another, and to understand how notes and chords fit together to form a melody or harmony.

écossaise (AY-koe-sayz, French). A country dance, perhaps of Scottish origin, popular in England and France in the 18th and 19th centuries. It is in a quick 2/4 time. Schubert and Beethoven both wrote *écossaises* for the piano.

eighth note. A note with a black head and with a flag attached to its stem, usually played or sung quickly. In quarter time, two *eighth notes* equal one count. In eighth time, one *eighth note* equals one count.

eighth rest. A sign instructing the performer to pause for a period equal in time to the length of one eighth note. *See* **notes and rests.**

eighth time. The time indicated when the number eight is the bottom number in the meter (or time) signature. One beat is given to each eighth note. The quarter note receives two beats; the half note, four beats, and so on.

einfach (INE-fahk, German). Play in a simple, direct way.

electric guitar. A steel guitar which is electrically powered. The instrument is attached by a cord to an outlet, the current from which operates a built-in electric

ELECTRIC GUITAR

speaker. The *electric guitar* is played like any other guitar, except that a volume knob controls loudness or softness of tone. Often used by dance bands.

elegy. Originally, a sad poem in memory of a loved one who has died. In music, a vocal or instrumental composition without words but with the same sad feeling.

embellishments. Musical ornaments such as turns, trills, runs, or other quick notes that decorate music and make it sound fuller.

embouchure (AHM-boo-sure, French). 1. The mouthpiece of wind instruments. 2. The correct way to form the lips to play a wind or brass instrument with a good tone.

encore (ON-kore, French). When a performer, at the end of his program, in response to the applause of his audience, repeats a number he has already played, or presents an additional piece, he gives an *encore.*

English horn. A double-reed woodwind instrument with a knob-shaped bell which is really an alto oboe. It is pitched in F, a fifth lower than the ordinary oboe

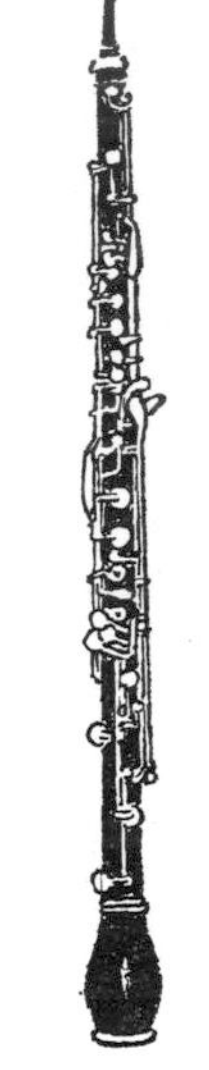

ENGLISH HORN

and its voice is deeper and fuller. It was first used in the middle of the 18th century. There is one *English horn* in a symphony orchestra.

enharmonic tones (en-har-MON-ic). Tones which sound the same but are written differently. Example: F♯ and G♭.

ensemble (en-SAHM-bel, French, "together"). In music a group of people playing, dancing, or singing together. A "good ensemble" means the players are giving a fine performance by working well together as a "team."

entr'acte (AHN-trakt, French, "between the acts"). Music played between the acts of an opera or play.

equal temperament. The division of a scale into twelve equal half steps or semitones.

Espagnol (Es-PAHN-yole, French). Describes music composed in a Spanish manner. Example: Albeniz's *Suite Espagnol* or Chabrier's *España.*

espressivo (es-pres-SEE-voh, Italian). Play or sing with feeling. (*abbrev.* esp.)

étude (EH-tyood, French, "study"). Music designed to help strengthen the fingers and improve technique, but written imaginatively so as to relieve the player of the boredom of dull scales or routine exercises. The *études* written by Chopin, Liszt, and Debussy are so beautiful that they are publicly performed. These compositions are sometimes called "Études de Concert."

étude de concert (EH-tyood de kon-SAIR, French). *See* **étude.**

exposition. The first section of a movement in sonata form. *See* **sonata form.**

expression. The feeling a performer gives to music when he plays or sings it. It is, in other words, the performer's interpretation of what the composer intended beyond the notes and directions of the score. These, to be sure, may tell him to play softly, firmly, gaily, rapidly, slowly, and so on; nevertheless, he is still left with a wide area of freedom in which to express himself and to make the music live.

expression signs. The composer's directions which are printed on the score. Composers began to use *expression signs* or directions 300 years ago. The person thought to have introduced them was an early 17th-century Italian musician, Domenico Mazzocchi, who included them in a book of madrigals. Because of their origin, many of the music signs in use today are written in Italian. (Examples: crescendo, forte, etc.) In the past fifty years, however, an increasing number of the signs have been written in French, German, and English. *See* **expression.**

F

facile (FAH-seel, French). Play or sing freely—with ease.

fagotto (fa-GOT-toe, Italian). A bassoon.

falsetto (fall-SET-toe, Italian). A method of singing in an unnatural high pitched voice above the adult male's normal range. Much used in early church music. (*abbrev.* falset.)

fanfare. Lively music for trumpets and kettle drums written mostly in triads. Usually played to announce an important event. Beethoven used a *fanfare* in his *Leonore Overtures.*

fantasia (fahn-TAH-zee-ah, Italian, "fancy"). Music in which the composer lets his imagination run free and does not write in strict form. An example is Bach's *Chromatic Fantasy and Fugue.*

F clef. A sign which indicates that the fourth line of the staff is to be read as F. Also known as the bass clef. *See* **bass clef.**

F holes. The sound-hole openings on the belly of the violin, viola, cello, and double bass which contribute to a better tone. The F-shape of the holes gives them their name.

fermata. A pause or hold. A note marked with a *fermata* may be held longer than its printed value. (Illus. p. xvi)

festival. A "feast" of music of all kinds. A series of musical performances held annually at a given place. *Festivals* such as those at Salzburg, Austria, and Tanglewood, Massachusetts are attended by musicians and audiences from all over the world. A long time ago, *festivals* were called "music conventions."

fiddle. A hillbilly nickname for a violin.

fiddler. One who plays a fiddle or violin.

fife. A small wood or metal wind instrument usually with one or more keys and with a range of two and one half octaves. It has six to eight finger holes and is played like the flute. Military bands are often famous for their *fife-and-drum* corps.

FIFE

filar la voce (fee-LAR la VO-chay, Italian, "draw out the voice"). Hold a tone evenly with the voice, gradually making it louder or softer.

filo de voce (FEE-loe de VO-chay, Italian). Sing with the softest and lightest possible tone.

finale (fee-NAH-lay, Italian). 1. In music, the last part or movement of a musical composition such as a symphony, sonata, concerto, or piece of chamber music. 2. The closing number of an opera or musical comedy. (*abbrev.* fin.)

fine (FEE-nay, Italian). The end of a piece of music. *See* ***da capo al fine*** and ***dal segno al fine.***

fine arts. A collective name for music, architecture, painting, sculpture, dancing, or other activities through which a person expresses his inner feelings or artistic convictions.

finger board. 1. The long thin strip of hard wood glued to the neck of stringed instruments. With the fingers of his left hand, the player presses the strings down upon the *finger board.* 2. A keyboard of a piano, organ, or accordion.

fingered. Describes music marked to show which fingers to use in playing the notes.

fingering. The proper use of the fingers in playing a musical instrument, as when pressing keys, strings, valves, or holes.

finger velocity. The ability to move the fingers quickly, with great power and facility when playing a musical instrument.

fioriture (fyor-i-TUR-eh, Italian). Extra notes or sounds, usually improvised by the player or singer. These notes embellish and decorate the music.

flageolet. A small wood or metal instrument of the recorder family. It has a mouthpiece like a whistle, six holes, and a range of about two and one half octaves. (*abbrev.* flag.)

FLAGEOLET

flat. A sign meaning to lower a tone one half step. *See* **accidentals.** (Illus. p. xvi)

flauto (fla-OO-toe). 1. A flute. 2. In an organ, one of the stops with a flutelike quality of tone.

fling. A gay and carefree dance in 4/4 time very much like a reel. Example: The Scottish Highland *fling.*

flue stops. 1. The flue pipe section of an organ which is divided into three groups: diapasons, flutes, and strings. 2. Also, the knobs or levers which regulate the flow of air into these pipes.

flute. A woodwind instrument formerly made of wood but now mostly of silver. It is shaped like a long, narrow tube and played while held horizontally by blowing across a mouth hole near one end. The *flute* has fourteen finger holes covered by keys. Its range is from B below middle C to the three octaves above, in the treble staff. It is a favorite obbligato instrument for piano and voice. *See* **obbligato.**

FLUTE

flutist (also **flautist**). A person who plays the flute.

folk dance. A dance originated by plain folk which expresses the way they live and work in their own communities. Most countries have their *folk dances,* which are usually performed in colorful native costumes. *See* **polka, Highland fling, cake walk, csardas, Virginia reel.**

folk song. A song handed down from generation to generation that tells stories of the work, lives, joys, and hardships of simple people. The authorship of *folk songs* is usually unknown.

form. The plan a composer uses to develop a melody and build harmonies in creating a composition. A *form* is for a composer what a plan is for an architect.

forte (FOR-tay, Italian, "strong"). Play loudly. (*abbrev.* f.)

fortepiano (FOR-tay-pee-AN-o, Italian, "loud-soft"). Play or sing a tone very loudly, then immediately get very soft. (*abbrev.* ff.)

fortissimo (for-TISS-i-mo, Italian). Play very loudly. (*abbrev.* ff.)

forza (FORT-sa, Italian). Usually, *con forza.* Play with push or vigor.

fox trot. A modern, two-step dance, fast or slow, in 4/4 time.

French horn. A brass wind instrument with a conical tube usually about 12 feet long, coiled in a circle. It has three valves and is played by blowing through a funnel-shaped mouthpiece and pushing down the valves. *French horn* music is written in the treble and bass clefs, and its range is three and a half octaves. A full symphony orchestra has five *French horns.*

French horn

fret. A narrow ridge of wood or metal crossing the neck part of the finger board of certain stringed instruments to mark the positions on which strings are stopped. The positions mark specific notes of the scale. Found on mandolins, guitars, zithers, lutes, and so on, but not on members of the violin family.

frog. *See* **nut.**

fugue. (fyoog, from the Italian *fuga,* "flight"). A musical version of follow-the-leader in which the lead voice enters and is then in effect imitated by the other voices in succession as each has its turn at presenting the melody. A *fugue* differs from a canon because the imitation occurs in shorter phrases or sections. In a canon the imitation of the melody is almost continuous.

full orchestra. A complete orchestra with all the customary instruments: strings, woodwinds, brass, and percussion instruments.

fuoco (foo-OH-co, Italian, "fire"). Play with fire and deep feeling.

G

gavotte (ga-VOT, French). An old French dance which gets its name from the inhabitants (the Gavots) of a certain section of France. The *gavotte* is written in 4/4 time, in two sections, each of which is repeated. It was introduced at the court of Louis XIV and was very popular until the time of the French Revolution.

G clef. The treble clef. A sign for higher sounds, it indicates that the second line of the staff is to be read as G. *See* **clef.**

Gesang (ge-SANG, German). A song.

gigue (JHEEG, perhaps from Old French *giga,* "fiddle"). A lively dance of the 17th and 18th centuries adapted from the jig. Usually with three, or some multiple of three, beats to the measure. Johann Sebastian Bach included *gigues* as the final movement of most of his keyboard suites. *See* **jig.**

giocoso (joe-KOE-soe, Italian, "jocose"). Play gaily.

giusto (JYOOS-toe, Italian, "just"). 1. Play in strict time. 2. Play in suitable tempo.

glee (from old English *gleo,* "music"). Sad or gay music for three or four unaccompanied male voices. Popular in England in the late 18th and early 19th centuries.

glee club. From the word "glee," referring to a group of persons who perform three- or four-part songs, usually accompanied by piano or other instruments. Most high schools and colleges have *glee clubs.*

glissando (glis-SAHN-doe, Italian). On stringed instruments, the effect made by sliding the finger along the strings very rapidly. On the piano, turning the thumb or forefinger on the nail and sliding it rapidly up or down the keys.

Trombones and string instruments play *glissando* in modern popular music.

glockenspiel (GLUK-en-shpeel, German). A set of bells tuned to a scale and sounded by striking with a hammer. The *glockenspiel* is also called the "orchestra bells."

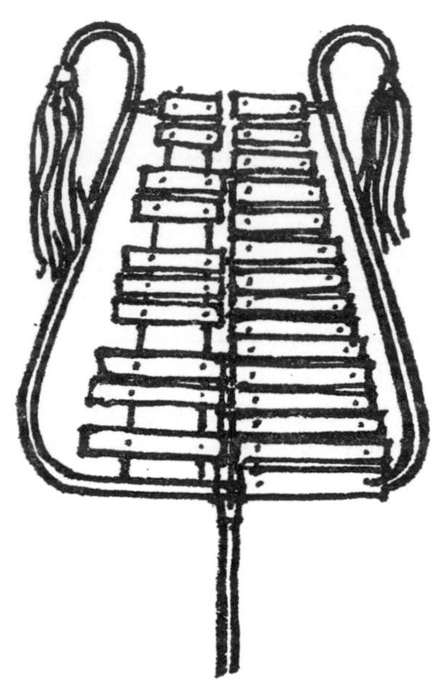

GLOCKENSPIEL

gopak. *See* ***hopak.***

gourds. A percussion instrument made of a dried tropical fruit shell. When shaken, the seeds inside the shell make a rattling sound. *Gourds* are used by rumba and samba bands to give their music a more exciting beat.

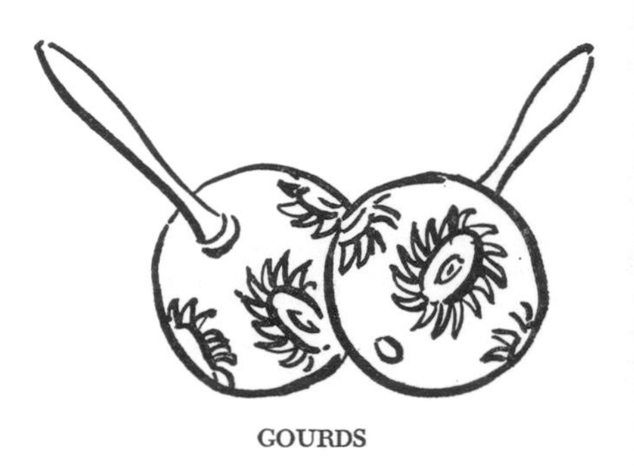

GOURDS

grace note. An extra note printed in much smaller type than ordinary notes of a musical score. *Grace notes* are meant to be musical decorations or ornaments and are played or sung without an extra count. In 17th- and 18th-century music, they often received the time representing an exact portion of the note to which they were attached.

grandioso (gran-dee-OH-so, Italian). Play or sing proudly, regally.

grave (GRAH-ve, Italian). Play slowly, solemnly, like funeral music.

grazioso (graz-ee-OE-soe, Italian). Play gracefully, with a lovely flow.

Gregorian chants (gre-GOR-ee-an). The most important extant collection of early church music, named after Pope Gregory I. A body of ancient hymns, the *Gregorian chants* were first arranged and codified at the end of the 6th century and became the most commonly used music in Roman Catholic church services.

grupetto (groo-PET-toe, Italian). An Italian name for "turn." Several quick notes played as a turn.

guitar. A fretted, wire- or gut-stringed instrument with a flat back and belly and a rounded waist. Its six strings are stopped on fret boards with the left-hand fingers, while the right hand strums and plucks them. Its music is written in the treble clef, but sounds an octave lower than that range. The *guitar* is used as a solo instrument, in background music for Spanish dancing and singing, for voice accompaniment in western and mountain folk singing, and in modern dance bands. It is of great antiquity and is thought to have been brought to Spain in the Middle Ages by the Moors.

guitarist. A guitar player.

gypsy music. Fiery, sad, or joyous music that sings of the life and adventures of the gypsies. It is easy to recognize through its minor sounds and the special type of minor scale used. Anton Dvořák used *gypsy music* in his Slavonic rhapsodies.

H

habanera (ah-bah-NAY-rah, Spanish). A slow Cuban dance, usually in 3/4 or 6/8 time but sometimes in 2/4 time. Popular in Spain in the 19th century, it is thought to have been imported there from Cuba.

half note. A white note with a stem. In quarter time the *half note* gets two counts; if there is a dot after the note, it get three counts. *See* **notes and rests.**

half rest. A sign instructing the performer to pause for a period equal in time to the length of one half note. *See* **notes and rests.**

hand position. The correct way to hold one's hands when playing an instrument.

harmonic mark. On a stringed instrument score, a small circle printed over a note. It is a direction to touch the string lightly, making a faint flutelike sound that is almost an echo of the main sound but an octave higher.

harmonica. Also called a mouth organ, this is a small wind instrument held between the fingers and played by inhaling or exhaling the breath. The *harmonica* has metal reeds of different sizes

HARMONICA

which, when set into vibration, produce various tones.

harmonium. A keyboard instrument of the reed-organ family developed by the Frenchman, C. J. Grenie, in the early 19th century, and perfected and patented in 1840 by A. Debain of Paris. The sounds of a *harmonium* are produced by reeds which vibrate when the player pumps the bellows pedals with his feet. Four or more stops act as controls for the sounds. A form of the *harmonium,* called the American organ or melodeon, was developed in the United States in the middle 1880's.

harmony. The art of combining musical tones in two, three, four or more note combinations. The word is also used to describe the study of chord functions, structures and relationships.

harp. The largest of the stringed instruments, dating from early pre-Christian times, triangular in shape with forty-six strings and seven pedals to shift the pitch of the strings. The *harp* in modern use was invented about 1820 by S. Erard. It is normally tuned in C-flat and has a range of over six octaves. Its pedals raise its sounds a half step or a whole step; this makes it possible to play in any key. Music for the *harp* is written in the treble and bass clefs. There are often two *harps* in a full symphony orchestra.

HARP

harpist. A person who plays the harp.

harpsichord. A principal ancestor of the piano and the favorite home keyboard instrument between the

HARPSICHORD

16th and 18th centuries. The *harpsichord* has two keyboards, one above the other, and its range is four octaves. Unlike the piano, whose strings are struck by hammers, those of the *harpsichord* are plucked by hard leather tongues or quills. Its characteristic delicate tone makes it an instrument which, to this day, gives pleasure to many people, especially when the original music written for it is played. Domenico Scarlatti wrote magnificent sonatas for the *harpsichord* in the 18th century.

harpsichordist. A harpsichord player.

hautboy (HO-boy, from French *hautbois*, "high wood"). The form of oboe used in the 17th and 18th centuries. *See* **oboe.**

HAUTBOY (OBOE)

Hawaiian guitar. A cousin of the guitar. The player holds the guitar on his knees. With one hand, he moves a small metal bar along the strings to make a slurring, gliding sound while the other hand plucks the strings with two or three picks. This guitar sounds very much like the dreamy, moving music of Hawaii.

head. 1. The tip of a stringed instrument bow for violin, viola, cello, or double bass. 2. Dried animal skin stretched over a banjo, tambourine, or drum. 3. The black or circle part of a note.

head voice (also **head tones**). The higher ranges of the singer's voice.

herzlich (HERZ-likh, German). Play or sing as from the heart.

hold. A sign (𝄐) over a note which means "hold it longer." *See* **fermata.**

homophonic. Refers to music in which chords accompany and support the melody. Think of a melody as a road over a bridge; then the *homophonic* chords are the pillars that support the road (or melody).

hopak (also ***gopak***). A lively Russian folk dance in 2/4 time. Moussorgsky wrote a *hopak* as a dance piece for the piano, and included one in an unfinished opera, *The Fair of Sorochintey.*

hora. A lively, popular Israeli dance in 4/4 time. Each dancer places his hands on his neighbor's shoulder and the group swings round in a circle.

hornpipe. Though one usually thinks of the *hornpipe* only in connection with sailors, it is in fact also

HORNPIPE

a country dance. Quick and very gay, popular in England from the 16th to the 19th centuries, *hornpipes* were once written in 3/4 time. By the 18th century they had evolved to 4/4 time. The dance gets its name from a rude instrument, a pipe made from the horn of an ox (mentioned by Chaucer).

hurdy-gurdy. 1. A mechanical instrument played by turning a crank. The "hurdy-gurdy man" with his monkey and his tin cup was a familiar sight on city streets at the beginning of this century. The instrument was usually rolled about on wheels but smaller ones were hung from the shoulders by leather straps. 2. A lute-shaped instrument, also played with a crank, with four to six strings,

HURDY-GURDY

two of which are melody strings, and the others drones. Popular in the 10th century, the *hurdy-gurdy* was once a highly respectable instrument played by serious musicians. After the 14th century, it lost its prestige and became the instrument of strolling players and beggars. In the 18th century, however, it again came into fashion, particularly in France. Haydn wrote five concertos and seven notturnos for *hurdy-gurdy*.

hymn. A song of praise to God, usually sung in a church. A *hymn* can also be a patriotic song. Example: "Battle Hymn of the Republic."

I

imitation. A type of musical composition in which one voice or instrument sings or plays a theme or melody, which is then repeated by a second voice or instrument. The repetition takes place while the first voice or instrument continues with the song; thus the two voices overlap. *Imitation* is used in rounds and fugues.

impresario (im-press-SAHR-ee-oe). A person who promotes and manages musical artists and orchestras. One of the best known modern impresarios is Sol Hurok.

impressionism. A school of composition which arose in the late 19th and early 20th centuries. It takes its name from the impressionist movement in painting, of which such artists as Monet and Renoir are famous examples. These painters were concerned more with the "impression" (that is, a mood or feeling) a scene makes upon a person looking at it than with a faithful reproduction of it as in a photograph. *Impressionism* in music is similar. The composer tries to express color and feeling and is less concerned with creating clear-cut melodies. For that reason, the music is not always easy to remember or hum. Impressionist composers often used the pentatonic or whole-tone scales which are very different from the conventional scales. Debussy, Ravel, and Griffes were well known musical impressionists.

impromptu. While the name *impromptu* suggests something improvised or made up on the spot, it was in fact used by romantic composers—Schubert, Chopin, Brahms among them—to describe short piano pieces which express moods or emotions.

improvise. To invent melodies and

harmonies while singing or playing an instrument.

incalzando (in-kal-TSAHN-doe, Italian). Press forward. Increase speed as you play.

incidental music. Songs or background music added to a play or film to set a mood, or to heighten excitement.

indeciso (in-de-CHEE-soe, Italian). Literally "undecided." Play as if without plan.

Indian music. Music created by the American Indians for magical purposes (rain dances for example) or for special ceremonies (such as weddings). It was frequently based on five-tone or sometimes, six-tone scales. The principal instruments used by the Indian musicians were a drum resembling a snare drum, a flute, and a rattle made from a gourd.

inner parts. In vocal music, the parts between the soprano and the bass.

instrumentalist. A player of a musical instrument.

instrumentation. 1. The way music is written or arranged or adapted for an orchestra or band. 2. The number and kinds of instruments used in an orchestra or band.

instruments. The devices which produce musical sounds. One may pluck or bow an *instrument* (the *stringed instruments*), blow into it (the woodwinds and brasses) or hit it (drums or other *percussion instruments*). The voice itself is a *musical instrument.*

brass instruments include: the trumpet, cornet, French horn, trombone, tuba, bugle.

percussion instruments with exact pitch, include: the bells, celesta, glockenspiel, chimes, kettle drum, xylophone, marimba, piano, and organ. Percussion instruments without exact pitch include: the snare drum, bass drum, tambourine, triangle, cymbals, castanets and gong. Also, rattles used in modern orchestral scores.

string instruments include: the violin, viola, cello, double bass, harp, mandolin, guitar, banjo, zither, dulcimer, koto, samisen, lute, etc.

woodwind instruments include: the flute, piccolo, English horn, oboe, bassoon, contra bassoon, clarinet, bass clarinet, recorder and saxophone. Although the saxophone is made of brass and the flute normally of silver, they, too, are classified as woodwind instruments.

intermezzo. Originally a short, lighthearted musical interlude, such as a song or madrigal, sandwiched between the acts of a play or opera. In time, the *intermezzo* became a short opera in two scenes, using two or three characters, still performed between the acts of a drama. By the 18th century, it broke away from the parent play and became a separate entertainment. The French *opéra comique* is an outgrowth of the *intermezzo* form. 2. A name used by Schumann and Brahms to describe short piano pieces, akin to impromptus.

interpretation. The feeling one expresses in performing a dance, or song, or playing an instrument. *See* **expression.**

interval. The distance or difference in pitch between two sounds. Two notes sounded at the same time produce a *harmonic interval;* two notes sounded one after another produce a *melodic interval. Intervals* may be measured from the lower tone to the higher tone. The smallest *interval* is called semitone or one half step. Example: g to G♯, b to c, d♭ to d. The *diatonic interval* is one whose upper note belongs to the major scale of the lower note. *Diatonic intervals* are divided into two groups, *major* and *perfect.* The *major intervals* are the second, third, sixth, seventh. The *perfect intervals* are the prime, fourth, fifth and octaves. The *chromatic interval* is one whose upper note does not belong to the major scale of the lower note. There are three groups of *chromatic intervals: minor, diminished, augmented.* A *minor interval* is formed only from a *major* by lowering the upper note one half step. A *diminished interval* is formed from a *minor* or *perfect interval* by lowering the upper tone one half step. An *augmented interval* is formed from a *major* or *perfect interval* by raising the upper tone one half step. Thirds and sevenths cannot be augmented.

intonation. The quality of singing or playing on the correct pitch. *Good intonation* means "in tune"; *bad intonation* means "out of tune."

introduction. The beginning of a musical composition. It may be a phrase, division, or entire section. Beethoven's second and seventh symphonies both have *introductions.*

inventions. The title of two sets of keyboard compositions written by Bach about 1723. Bach called the first set "Inventiones," the second set "Sinfonie." The "Inventiones," which are studies in two-part counterpoint, are also known as the "Two Part Inventions." The "Sinfonies," which are also studies in counterpoint, are known as "Three Part Inventions."

inversion. Reversing the positions of the tones of an interval or chord so that the bottom tone becomes the top tone. When inverted, most intervals are changed as follows: A major interval becomes minor. A minor interval becomes major. A diminished interval becomes augmented. An augmented interval becomes diminished. Only a perfect interval remains a perfect interval. Triads have two *inversions*. Example: The *first inversion* of the C major triad (CEG) is EGC; the *second inversion*, GCE.

Irish pipe. The Irish cousin of the bagpipe, with a softer tone. At first the Irish pipe was played like a Scottish bagpipe (by blowing into it), but later was played by squeezing a bellows placed under the arm.

-issimo. "Very." Example: *Pianissimo* means very softly.

J

jam session. In jazz, a group of performers playing improvised arrangements, usually for their own entertainment.

jarabe (hah-RAH-bay). A lively Mexican dance, resembling a mazurka. It was brought to Mexico from Spain, where it is believed to have been performed by Andalusian gypsies.

jazz. Modern syncopated music with a swing to it. One can dance to it, sing it, or simply listen to it. The name is sometimes said to have come from "Jasbo" Brown, a Negro musician who lived on the Mississippi in the last century.

JAZZ

jew's-harp. An instrument shaped like a horseshoe with a metal tongue between its two ends. The player holds it between his lips while twanging the metal tongue

JEW'S-HARP

with his finger. The *jew's-harp* is an ancient instrument found in many parts of the world, and is known by many names. It has nothing to do with the Jewish people. Instead, its name is thought to be a corruption of "jaw's harp," that is, a harp held between the jaws.

jig. A country dance in 6/8 time performed with a quick "1-2" rhythm. Today, *jig* usually means "Irish jig," a lively dance full of the humor and high spirits of the Irish. In the 16th century, however, it was well known in England and Scotland. The gigue, which became popular on the Continent in the 17th and 18th centuries, developed from the 16th-century *jig*.

jongleur (zhon-GLOOR, French). A minstrel, or professional musician of the Middle Ages, who often asisted the troubadour. *See* **minstrel.**

jota (HOE-tah, Spanish). A quick Spanish dance for couples in 3/4 time. Often accompanied by guitar and castanets. Popular in northern Spain.

jubilee. A celebration or festival, with music and singing, in honor of a special event or anniversary.

K

Kapellmeister (kah-PEL my-stur, German). Conductor of an orchestra or choir.

kettledrum. Also known as the timpanum (pl. timpani). A bowl-shaped percussion instrument, with a dried animal skin (called "parchment") stretched over the top and held in place by an iron ring. It is tuned by a set of hand screws or a pedal attachment and is the only drum with definite pitch. The sticks used to play the *kettledrum* have soft knobs made of lamb's wool or sponge. The instrument stands on a metal tripod or wheeled carriage. Orchestras use three different *kettledrums.* The *high kettledrum* has a range from the bass staff C to G. The *medium kettledrum* has a range from the first leger line below the bass staff E♭ to B♭. The *low kettledrum* has a range from the first leger line below the bass staff to G. All *kettledrum* music is printed on the bass staff.

KETTLE DRUMS

key. 1. On the keyboard instruments (piano, organ, accordion, etc.) a wooden lever, covered with ivory or a plastic substance which when struck or pushed, controls the mechanism which produces sound. A piano keyboard has thirty-six black *keys* and fifty-two white *keys.* Each *key* is attached to a hammer. When the *key* is pressed, the hammer strikes a string, thus making a sound. (*See* ***piano, harpsichord, organ.***) 2. On many wind instruments, a flat lever made of a leather-padded metal disc which covers a sound hole. The finger works the level to open or close the sound hole.

keyboard. 1. The long wooden board under the keys of a piano, organ, or accordion, on which the white and black keys rest. 2. The entire set of keys on a piano or a *keyboard* instrument.

key note. The first or tonic note of a scale. For example, D is the *key note* (or first note) of a scale in the key of D.

key signature. A sign which indicates the key, or "sound family" in which the music is written. It consists of a group of sharps or flats placed between the clef and the time signature. Each key has its own signature. For example, the signature of the key of D major, is two sharps, F♯ and C♯. When the performer sees this signature he knows that he will be playing in the key of D major (or its related minor) and that every time he sees an F or C in the score, he must sharp them.

koto (koe-toe). A long zither-like instrument with thirteen strings, used for both solo and ensemble work. It is popular in Japan where many children take *koto* lessons. Normally a *koto* player performs while seated on the floor.

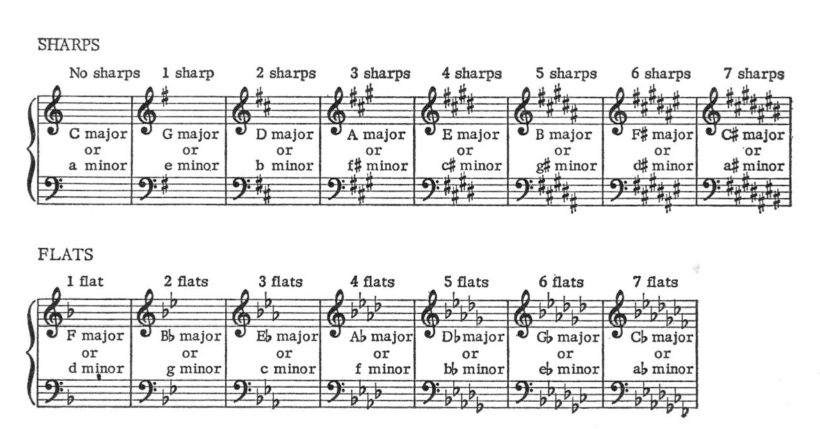

MAJOR AND MINOR KEY SIGNATURES

krakowiak (kra-KAW-yah, Polish). A Polish group dance in quick

2/4 time performed with much shouting and hitting at the heels. It was danced for happy occasions such as weddings or birthdays. Popular in the 19th century.

L

Ländler (LEND-ler, German). A slow Austrian waltz danced either in 3/4 or 3/8 time. Beethoven and Schubert wrote many *Ländler* which were popular in the early 19th century.

langsam (LAHNG-sahm, German, "slowly"). Play or sing slowly. *Lento.*

largamente (lahrga-MEN-teh, Italian). Play or sing slowly and broadly. (*abbrev.* larg.)

larghetto (lahr-GET-toe, Italian). *See* **largo.**

largo (LAR-goe, Italian). Slow, serious, and dignified. Thus, also, *larghetto,* a diminutive: not quite as slow as largo.

leader. Conductor of an orchestra, choir or band.

leading melody. The main song or theme.

leading tone. The seventh note of the scale, which leads to the principal note, by a semitone. In everyday language, the seventh tone is "trying to push" to the eighth, which is "home."

l.h. Abbreviation for "left hand." Its appearance in a piano score means that the music so marked should be played with the left hand. This usually requires crossing the left hand over the right while playing.

legatissimo (le-ga-TIS-see-moe, Italian). Very legato. Play very smoothly and evenly, in as connected a manner as possible.

legato (le-GAH-toe, Italian, "connected"). Play or sing smoothly, without pause or break, in passing from tone to tone. (*abbrev.* leg.)

leger lines (ledg-er). The short lines drawn above, below and between the treble and bass staffs. On them are printed the notes that are pitched too high or too low to be printed in the staff itself.

leggiero (lej-YAIR-oe, Italian, "lightly"). Give the music a light, floating feeling, as if sailing on a cloud.

leicht (liehkt, German, "lightly"). Play with a light touch.

leitmotiv (LIET-moe-teef, German). A melody repeated many times in an opera to identify a character, evoke an idea, or illustrate a particular event in the story. When the *leitmotiv* is played, the actor or event with which it is associated takes over the main action on the stage. One of the greatest composers of opera, Richard Wagner, often used this musical device.

lento (LEN-toe, Italian). Play slowly. Tempo between andante and largo.

librettist (li-BRET-tist). A person who writes a libretto. *See* **libretto.**

libretto (li-BRET-toe, Italian, "little book"). The text of an opera or musical show, that is, the words sung or recited which tell the story.

lieder (LEE-der, German, "songs.") Most often the name refers to the romantic songs of Schubert, Schumann, Brahms, and Hugo Wolf.

Lieder ohne Worte (LEE-der own-ne VOR-te, German, "songs without words.") Felix Mendelssohn wrote many "songs without words" for the piano.

lipping. In wind instrument playing, adjusting the lips to bring the note in tune or give it better quality.

loco. A direction to disregard a previous "8va" marking and to play the notes as written.

loud pedal. The damper or right foot pedal on a piano. Used to give the music a richer, more flowing sound. *See* **damper pedal.**

loure (loor, French). Originally, a kind of French bagpipe. Later, about the 17th century, the name came to mean a slow dance in 6/4 or 3/4 time. *Loures* were included in operas and in instrumental suites.

lullaby. A soft, gentle song sung by a mother to lull her child to sleep.

lustig (LOOS-tig, German). Play merrily.

lute (loot). A stringed instrument having a pear-shaped body, a long neck with a fretted finger board and multiple sets of strings to be plucked with the fingers. The *long lute* was probably the older instrument and was used in early Egypt and the Near East. The *short lute* appeared in Spain in the 10th century. By the 15th century, it was the most widely used European instrument played by troubadours and minstrels and it acquired a large repertory of music for solo performance and for song accompaniment. It flourished in the 17th and early 18th centuries through Bach's time. It

LUTE

was then put aside for the more easily tuned guitar.

lyre (lire). A very old string instrument, grandfather of the modern harp. Its two arms curved above a sound box and were connected with a crossbar over which the strings were stretched. It was much smaller than the harp, with three to twelve strings, and it could be easily carried. In ancient times, Israel, Babylonia, and Egypt had various kinds of *lyres*.

LYRE

lyric (LEER-ik) (from the Greek word *lyra*, "to sing"). 1. Describes a short, sweet song with a beautiful melody. 2. Also describes instrumental music which has a singing quality.

lyric drama. Words and music combined to make an opera or a musical show.

lyrics. Words set to music, usually in an opera or a musical show. In popular music, also the words of a song.

M

ma (Italian, "but"). Example: *ma non troppo* means "but not too much."

madrigal. A type of vocal music for several voices. Two main kinds have evolved. In 14th-century Italy a *madrigal* followed an established form: it was a short poem of eight or eleven lines, set to music for two or three unaccompanied voices. In 16th-century Italy *madrigal* came to have a second meaning: polyphonic unaccompanied vocal music, free in form, written for several voices. The popularity of these songs spread throughout Europe and to England, where by the end of the 16th century a famous school of *madrigal* composers had arisen. Today, *madrigal* societies still delight audiences all over the world.

maestoso (my-STOE-soe, Italian). Play or sing in a dignified, majestic manner. Think of a king entering a throne room. (*abbrev.* maest.)

maestro (my-ES-troe, Italian, "master"). A leader or conductor of music, particularly a musician whose experience and skill are rare and outstanding. Thus the conductor Arturo Toscanini was called *Maestro.*

Magnificat. The hymn to the Virgin Mary, sung as part of the Vesper services in the Roman Catholic church. A musical form used in the early polyphonic school, it is always written to the St. Luke i 46-55 text, "My soul doth magnify the Lord." Two of the most beautiful *Magnificats* were written by Johann Sebastian Bach and Karl Philipp Bach. A modern *Magnificat* has been written by the British composer, Ralph Vaughn Williams.

main (man, French). The hand.

main droite (man dwaht, French). The right hand. (*abbrev.* M.D.)

main gauche (man goe-sh, French). The left hand. (*abbrev.* M.G.)

major scale. A succession of eight tones arranged in a pattern of whole and half steps. The half steps fall between the third and fourth tones and the seventh and eighth tones. Each half of the scale (four degrees) is called a "tetrachord." Both lower and higher tetrachords are separated by a whole step.

mandolin. A small, pear-shaped, stringed instrument of the lute family, usually with four double strings. It is tuned like a violin and is played by plucking the strings with a pick or plectrum. It has a range of about three octaves beginning on the G below middle C. Originating in Italy and Spain, it has been in use since the 18th century.

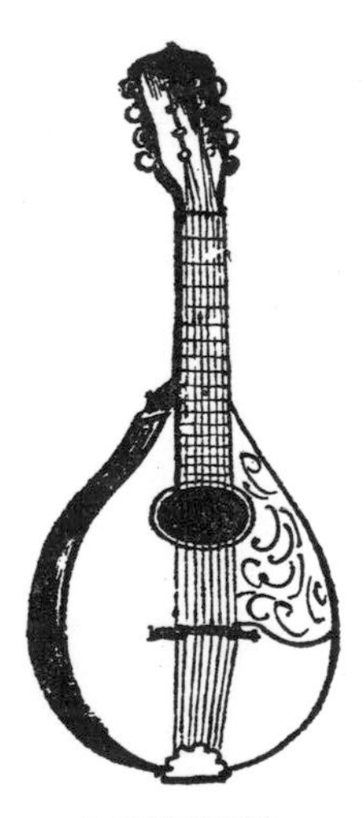

MANDOLIN

mano (Italian). The hand.

mano destra (MAHN-oe DES-trah, Italian). The right hand. (*abbrev.* m.d.)

mano sinistra (MAHN-oe sin-EES-trah, Italian). The left hand. (*abbrev.* m.s.)

manual. 1. A hand-played keyboard of the organ. 2. In organ music, a direction to play with the hands only, without using the pedals.

marcato (mahr-KAH-toe, Italian). In a marked, decisive manner. Bring the tone out more. (*abbrev.* marc.)

march. Music with a military rhythm to it, which can be brisk or grave, written in very strict, duple meter time (2/4, 4/4, 6/8, played in two beats; 12/8 played in four beats). In Mexico, the *paso doble*—a type of march—is in 3/4 time.

marimba (mah-RIM-bah, from the African word *marimba* or *malimba*—the plural of *limba*)." A percussion instrument that looks like a xylophone, but is much larger. Its range is five octaves. It is sounded by striking wooden blocks of different lengths with small wooden hammers which

MARIMBA

create a bell-like sound. Used widely in Mexico, but originally came from Africa.

masque (mask, French). A dramatic entertainment, forerunner

MASQUE

of the modern opera, which combined poetry, music, and dancing and was performed with elaborate costumes and scenery. *Masques* were favorite diversions of the nobility of the 16th and 17th centuries, particularly in England.

Mass. The principal worship service of the Roman Catholic church, portions of which (Kyrie, Gloria, Credo, Sanctus, Benedictus and Agnus Dei) are often set to polyphonic music. Other parts are sung in Gregorian chant or spoken. When the Kyrie, Gloria, Credo, Sanctus, Benedictus and Agnus Dei are set to music, they are known collectively as a *Mass.*

mazurka (mah-ZUR-kah). A national Polish dance which dates from the 16th century, set in 3/4 or 3/8 time with strong accents on the second and third beats. It is sometimes lively, sometimes sad. Chopin wrote fifty-two *mazurkas* for the piano.

measure. 1. The section of staff space marked off by vertical bars between which notes are written. The purpose of a *measure* is to help you play or sing with the same sure, steady beat over and over again until the end of the music. 2. A stately dance, resembling a pavane or minuet, performed in the 15th and 16th centuries.

medieval music. The music written from about 500 A.D. to about 1450.

Meistersingers (MY-stir-singers, German, "master singers"). Guilds or societies of musicians that flourished in Germany in the 15th and 16th centuries. The members, who were masters of their craft, devoted themselves to encouraging the development of German poetry, music, and musical knowledge. The finest singers among them were given prizes in recognition of their accomplishments. Richard Wagner wrote a famous and frequently performed opera called *The Meistersingers of Nuremberg*, first produced in in 1868. It is a true story of these early music guilds.

melodeon. The first small reed organ used in the United States over 100 years ago. Much like an early harmonium, it had a range of six octaves.

MELODEON

melodrama. Originally, a serious drama in which the orchestra played a musical accompaniment as an actor spoke his lines. Today the name describes a mystery, or a play with other forms of suspense and excitement. There may or may not be a musical background to heighten the effect.

melody. 1. A succession of notes which are pleasant and tuneful. 2. A tune or song with instrumental accompaniment.

meno mosso (MEN-oe MOE-soe, Italian, "less motion"). Play or sing more slowly.

meter. The pattern of strong and weak counts or beats in a piece of music. The pattern is repeated over and over from the beginning of the piece to the end. *Duple* (or 2/4) *meter* has a "strong, weak" beat. *Triple* (or 3/4) *meter* has a "strong, weak, weak" beat.

meter signature. The number sign at the beginning of a composition. The top number tells you how many beats there are in each measure. The bottom number tells you what kind of a note gets one beat. For example: In 3/4 meter, the 3 means there are three beats to a measure and the 4 means a quarter note gets one beat; in 6/8 meter, the 6 means there are six beats to a measure and the 8 means an eighth note gets one beat.

metronome. A mechanical device, originally constructed to help a composer indicate the pace at which his work was to be performed, now mainly used as a time keeper for a student practicing his music. The *metronome* had the attention of many early

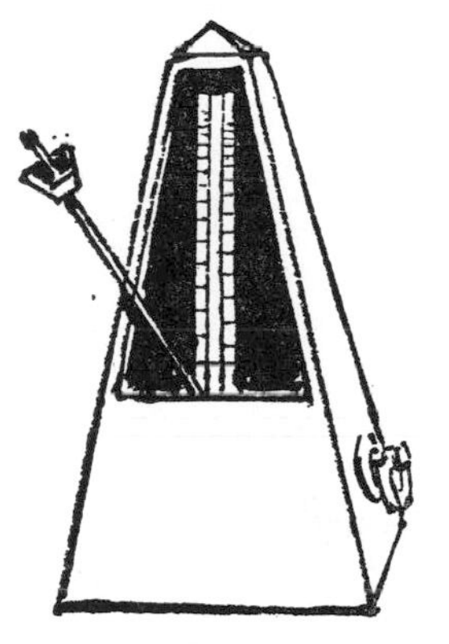

METRONOME

inventors, and was brought more or less to its present form in 1816 by J. N. Maelzel. It is a small machine, the most important part of which is a 7-inch long steel rod suspended by a pivot in a wooden case, with a fixed weight at the bottom end of the rod and a sliding weight at the upper end. By a clock spring or an electrical mechanism the rod is made to swing back and forth, while giving out a ticking sound. Adjustment of the sliding weight makes the rod swing slower or faster, corresponding to the tempo of the music.

mezzo (MET-soe, Italian). Half. For example ***mezzo forte*** means "half loud."

mezzo forte (MET-soe FOR-teh, Italian). Play or sing half as loud as forte, or fairly loud. (*abbrev.* mf.)

mezzo piano (MET-soe pee-AH-noe, Italian). Play or sing half as soft as piano, or fairly soft. (*abbrev.* mp.)

mezzo-soprano (MET-soe so-PRAH-noe, Italian). The female voice with a range halfway between soprano and alto. A *mezzo-soprano* can sing from the first A below middle C to high F on the fifth line in the treble staff.

middle C. The C-note near the middle of the piano keyboard. It is printed as the first leger line below the treble staff or the first leger line above the bass staff.

military band. A group of musicians, usually in uniform, who play military music on woodwind, brass, and percussion instruments.

military music. Music written for a military band. The clarinets in the band take the place of the violins in the orchestra, with the result that there are many more clarinet players in a military band than in an orchestra.

minnesingers (MIN-ne-singers, German). German poets and musicians who lived in the 12th to 14th centuries. They were as important to the growth of German creative art as the troubadours were to French creative art. *See* **troubadour.**

minor scale. A succession of eight tones, arranged in a pattern of whole and half steps, in which the third tone is a half step lower than that of a major scale. *See* **relative minor scale.**

minstrel (Sometimes called a jongleur). 1. The name was originally applied to a musician of the 14th century who was often an attendant to a troubadour, accompanying him on a stringed instrument. Some *minstrels* were employed as permanent entertainers in the courts of wealthy nobles. Others were wanderers who traveled from town to town singing and spreading the news. 2. Today a *minstrel* is a white entertainer in Negro make-up. Tom Rice, a white comedian, performed a solo song-and-dance act in blackface in 1828, and is known as the father of American minstrelsy. Stephen Foster wrote many of his famous songs such as "Old Folks at Home" and "Jeanie with the Light Brown Hair" for a *minstrel* group known as "Christy's Minstrels."

MINSTREL

minuet (min-yoo-ET). A gracious and stately French dance in 3/4 time, very popular in the courts of Europe in the 17th and 18th centuries. 2. Sometimes, a movement of a classical sonata or symphony.

miracle plays. Stories from the Bible or the lives of the saints acted out with songs or musical accompaniment. Popular in the Middle Ages.

misterioso (mis-ter-ee-OE-so, Italian). Make the music "spooky"—full of suspense and mystery.

M.M. (An abbreviation for Maelzel's Metronome). The letters

M.M. are usually found at the upper left hand corner of a page of music, and indicate the setting of the metronome.

mode. The way intervals are arranged to form a scale. The *major* or *minor mode* means the way in which these scales are put together. *See* **major scale, minor scale.**

moderato (mah-der-AH-toe, Italian). Play or sing at a moderate, easy speed. A musical direction.

modern music. Music written by composers who broke away from the impressionist school about fifty or sixty years ago. They wished to experiment with musical expression in new and unexplored ways. The modern composers use many different forms or structures in their work and write in different styles one of which is *expressionism,* in which they avoid a basic key or tonality, or use a twelve-tone system of composition. Arnold Schoenberg is famous for his twelve-tone works. Another style is *neoclassicism,* in which the composer returns to the classical musical form but translates it into "modern" sounds. Igor Stravinsky, Bela Bartok, and Paul Hindemith are examples of this group of composers. There are many other groups which are classified as modern composers. There are, for example, the nationalists who try to compose music which expresses the political feeling of their country. Dmitri Shostakovich and Sergei Prokofiev, both Russians, are examples of this group. Others, such as the Americans Morton Gould, Charles Ives, Aaron Copland, and Leonard Bernstein, try to catch the excitement of our times.

modulation. 1. A change of key effected by passing through a succession of chords. 2. A shift from one key to another key by the use of a chord or chords common to both keys.

molto (MOL-toe, Italian). Very, or much more.

molto adagio (MOL-toe A-DAH-jyo, Italian). Play or sing much more slowly.

molto vivace (MOL-toe vee-VAH-chay, Italian). Play or sing in a very lively manner.

monody (from two Greek words: *monos,* "one"; *oide,* "song"). A composition for one voice. The term sometimes describes an unaccompanied solo.

monophonic (from two Greek words: *monos,* "one"; *phone,* "sound"). Describes music sung by one voice without accompaniment. A Gregorian chant is *monophonic* music.

monotone. 1. A single tone. 2. Words recited on a single tone.

mordent. A musical ornament played by alternating the written note with the note below or above it. It receives part of the time value of the printed note.

morendo (moe-REN-doe, Italian). Let the sound gradually die away, like a train whistle growing softer in the distance. (*abbrev.* mor.)

mosso (MOE-soe, Italian). Move. For example, *Più mosso* means "make this move much more."

motive (also **motif**). A short musical phrase consisting of a few notes that reappears in a composition. It is like an incomplete phrase of a sentence.

moto (MOE-toe, Italian). Play with motion or animation.

mountain songs. Narrative songs that originated among the mountain peoples of the United States. A *mountain song* may be a ballad, a love song, a song of loneliness or sadness. Together with cowboy songs, railroad songs and work songs, they form the folk music of this country.

MOUNTAIN SONGS

mouth harmonica. *See* **harmonica.**

mouthpiece. The part of a wind instrument held against the player's lips or inserted in his mouth.

movement. A major part or section of a musical composition, such as a sonata or symphony. Most symphonies have four *movements.*

musette. 1. A soft-toned bagpipe popular in France in the 17th and 18th centuries. Bach imitated the *musette* in his dance suites for the piano. 2. A country dance in 2/4, 3/4 or sometimes 6/8 time originally written for a *musette. Musettes* were fashionable at the 18th-century court.

music box. A mechanical music-making device wound like a clock or cranked like a hurdy-gurdy consisting of a pin-studded metal cylinder which is rotated against a row of metal teeth. As the cylinder turns, the pins strike or twang the teeth, each of which produces a different tone. *Music boxes,* which were invented more than 100 years ago, were often made in elaborate and versatile forms. For example they incorporated metal discs which could be changed like phonograph records, and which played different tunes. Ornamented boxes had small figures which danced to the music. Switzerland is known for its finely-crafted *music boxes.*

music critic. A writer for a newspaper or magazine who reviews concerts. The *music critic's* job is to listen to a performance, judge it, and report his opinion to his readers. A few critics are performers themselves, and most have studied music and have a thorough knowledge of the subject.

music hall. A large hall or auditorium where musicians and entertainers perform.

music typography. The printing of notes and musical symbols.

musical comedy. A gay, brightly costumed play with singing and dancing. Nowhere has the *musical comedy* been pursued with more energy and inventiveness than in the United States.

musicale. A musical performance given in a private home.

musician. A person trained to perform, conduct, compose, or teach music.

musicologist. A specialist in musical knowledge. He is concerned with the history, theory, philosophy, and psychology of music in all its forms. Usually he is an author, teacher, or lecturer.

mute. 1. A pronged device fitted to the bridge of a bow-stringed instrument (such as a violin) to soften the music. 2. A "muzzle" put in the opening of a horn or trumpet to soften its sound.

muting. Muffling or deadening a sound with a mute.

N

Nachtmusik (NAHKT-moo-zeekk, German, "night music"). An evening song or instrumental composition; a serenade.

narrator. In music, a person who tells a story while music is being played. The story and the tunes combine into a musical narrative. An excellent example of narrated music is Prokofiev's *Peter and the Wolf.*

national music. Music written about a nation or a country.

natural. The sign (♮) which tells you to cancel the previous sharp or flat. It directs the performer to play the original note. (Illus. p. xvi)

natural scale. The scale of C, which has no sharps or flats.

neck. The long, thin, projecting portion of a stringed instrument on which the finger board and upper parts of the strings are fixed.

nocturne. Quiet, flowing, dreamlike, romantic music, often describing the night. Chopin wrote many beautiful *nocturnes* for piano.

noel (noe-ELL, French, Christmas). A Christmas carol. *See* **carol.**

non (French or Italian, "not"). Examples: *Non legato* means "not smoothly." *Ma non troppo* means "but not too much." *Non tanto* means "not too much."

notation. The printed signs used in music such as: the staff, notes, rests, clefs, bars, time signatures, key signatures, dots, ties, slurs, and so forth.

notes and rests. Written symbols showing the length of a musical sound or pause. The *note* symbol has two parts: the head, which sits or hangs on a line or space of the staff; and the stem. When two or more *notes* are grouped together, the connecting top line is

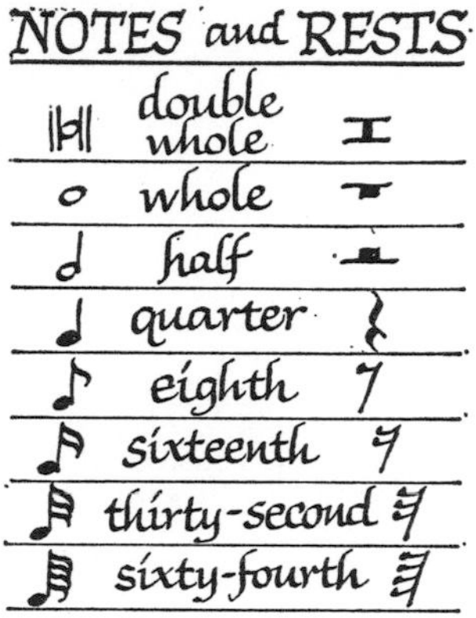

NOTES and RESTS

double whole
whole
half
quarter
eighth
sixteenth
thirty-second
sixty-fourth

called a "bridge" or "bar."

notturno (nah-TUR-noe, Italian). *See* **nocturne.**

numbered measure. A measure in which a number is printed which tells the musician how many measures he must count out and rest before it is his turn to play again.

nuptial music. Music for weddings. Mendelssohn's "Wedding March" from *A Midsummer Night's Dream* is a good example of *nuptial music.*

nut. 1. A ridge of raised ebony near the top of the neck of a stringed instrument. It helps hold in place the strings which pass over it after leaving the pegs. 2. The movable cylinder at the lower end of a bow to which the hair is attached. Turning the *nut* loosens or tightens the bow hairs. The *nut* is sometimes known as the "frog."

O

obbligato (ob-li-GAH-toe, Italian, "obliged"). 1. A part in a piece of music that cannot be left out, since it must be played to make the music complete. 2. Through some strange error, the term has also come to mean an accompanying part that may be left out if necessary. (*abbrev.* obb.)

oboe (OE-boe, from French *hautbois,* "high wood"). A high-pitched woodwind instrument descended from the shepherds' pipes, 26 inches long, with a double reed and finger holes and keys. When air is blown through the instrument, the double reed, which consists of two strips of cane bound together, helps create a thin penetrating sound. The orchestra is always tuned to the "a" sounded by the *oboe.* Its music is printed in the treble clef. Four *oboes* are used in a symphony orchestra. (*abbrev.* ob.)

OBOE

ocarina (ah-kah-REE-nah, from the Italian *oca,* "goose"). A wind instrument made of metal or earthenware shaped like a goose or a sweet potato. It has a number of finger holes and is played by blowing into a mouthpiece. The *ocarina* is sometimes called a "sweet potato" because of its shape.

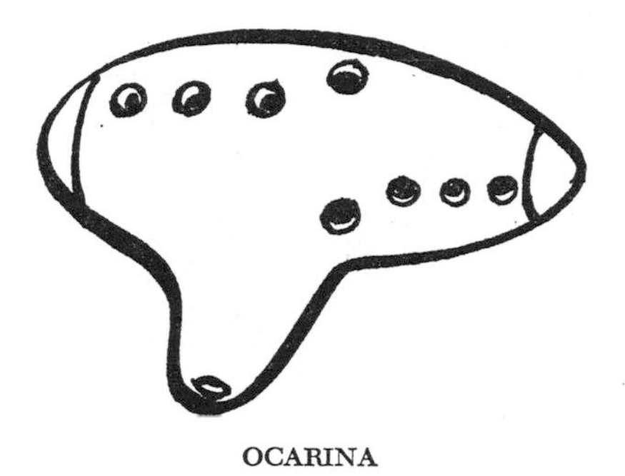

OCARINA

octave. The interval between a tone and the tone above or below it that has the same key name. In other words, the interval between the first and eighth (or last) tone of a major or minor scale. Example: Middle C to the C above it.

octet. Music written for eight instruments or voices.

open pedal. The damper, or right pedal. *See* **damper pedal.**

open string. A string is called "open" when it is unstopped, that is, when the fingers of the left hand do not press down on it. An *open string* vibrates its full length.

opera (AH-per-ah, from the Italian *opera in musica,* "work in music"). A play set to music for singers and orchestra, usually performed with elaborate scenery and costumes. Among the principal forms are: *grand opera,* a serious, usually tragic, drama in which the dialogue is sung rather than spoken; *opéra bouffe,* a comic drama, also sung throughout; *opéra comique,* which mingles spoken dialogue with singing; *singspiel,* a German version of the French *opéra comique.*

operetta (ah-per-ET-tah, Italian). A little or shorter opera, gay and light, and with tunes easy to whistle or hum. Usually an *operetta* contains some spoken parts.

opus (OE-puss, Latin, "work"). A composition or group of compositions. The word *opus* in music is most frequently used together with numbers to identify the chronological order in which a composer has written and published his works. Thus, for example, *Opus No. 1* designates a composer's first published composition. (*abbrev.* op.)

oratorio (or-a-TOR-ee-oe, from Latin *oratio,* "speech"). A composition for solo voices, orchestra, and chorus, which tells a story but is performed without scenery or costumes. *Oratorios,* which are almost always on religious subjects, resemble cantatas, but are usually considerably longer.

orchestra (Greek, "dancing place"). Originally, the *orchestra* was the part of the Greek theater reserved for dance and instrumental per-

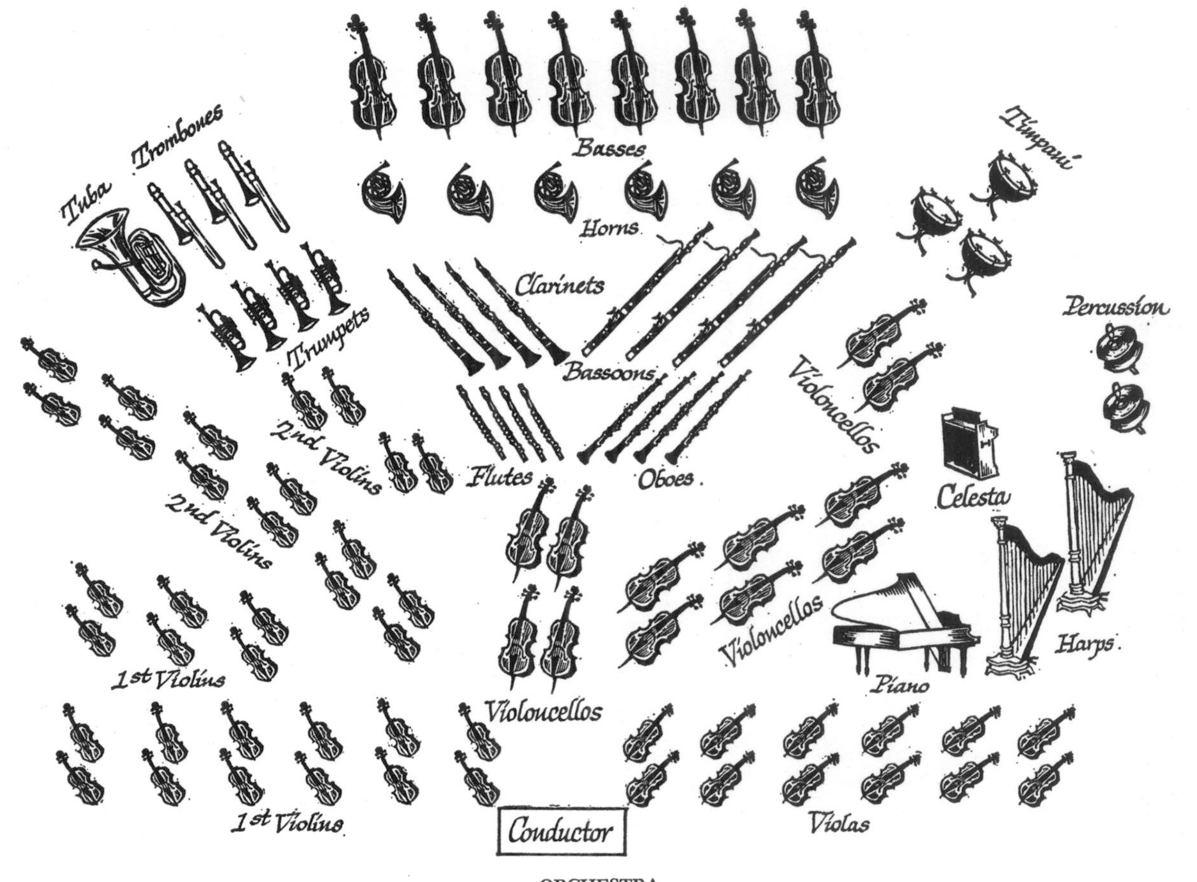
Tuba
Trombones
Basses
Timpani
Horns
Trumpets
Clarinets
Bassoons
Percussion
Violoncellos
2nd Violins
Flutes
Oboes
Celesta
2nd Violins
Violoncellos
Harps
1st Violins
Piano
Violoncellos
1st Violins
Conductor
Violas

ORCHESTRA

formances. Now it is a group of musicians led by a conductor, playing string, brass, woodwind, and percussion instruments. The size of an orchestra can vary from a small ensemble to a full symphony group of about 100 musicians. Orchestras began as much smaller groups in the opera houses of the 17th century.

orchestral. Having to do with an orchestra or the instruments of an orchestra.

orchestration. The art of scoring for an orchestra, so that the composition can be played by all the instruments. The orchestral score, as we know it today, originated in the 17th century.

organ. A large keyboard wind instrument, many centuries old, which because of its versatility, size, power, and quality is known as the "king" of musical instruments. The modern *organ* is a formidable mechanism, consisting of pipes and keyboards. There are two main pipe sections, flue pipes and reed pipes, which can be played separately or together. Sound is produced by forcing air through the pipes, the air being controlled by stops, which are push-and-pull buttons lined up in front of the player. There are up to 100 stops on the modern *organ.* No less elaborate are the keyboards. As many as seven different hand-played keyboards, one above the other, called manuals, may be found in today's *organ;* below is a pedal keyboard played with the feet. In the electronic *organ*, a comparatively recent invention, sound is produced by electrical impulses rather than by air pressure.

ORGAN

overture. 1. Instrumental music played as an introduction to an opera or musical play. The *overture* usually includes melodies from the main songs to follow. 2. An independent piece of instrumental music for an orchestra, not associated with an opera or play. Examples: *Fingal's Cave* by Mendelssohn; Brahms' *Tragic Overture.*

P

paraphrase. The arrangement, which is to say, the rewriting or elaboration of music written for one instrument or voice for another instrument or voice, with changes in melody, rhythm, or harmony. Variations of the melody can also be added. *See* **variations.**

part. The line of music assigned to each voice or instrument. A *part* may be performed as a solo or by a group of identical voices or instruments. For example, in a string quartet, one viola plays the viola *part.* In an orchestral work, all of the violas play the viola *part.*

partita (par-TEE-tah, Italian). A 17th- and 18th-century title for a set of variations or dances. 2. In early classical music, a suite. Bach's six *partitas* for the piano and three *partitas* for unaccompanied violin are really dances grouped as a suite.

part singing. Singing part-song music *a capella*—or in a group, usually with no accompaniment.

part song. Music written for at least three harmonizing voices with no accompaniment.

pas (pah, French). A step in a dance, or, as in *pas de deux*, a dance for two.

passacaglia (pah-sah-KAL-yah, Italian). In the 17th century a composition for a keyboard instrument, slow and stately, in 3/4 time, similar to the chaconne. A *passacaglia* is characterized by a short bass theme which is repeated in many variations. Both Buxtehude and Bach wrote *passacaglias* for the organ. Bach's *Passacaglia in C Minor* is considered a masterpiece. The form is still used in contemporary music; the 20th-century American composer, Walter Piston, has written a *passacaglia* for the piano.

passage. 1. A short section of a musical composition. 2. A section in which a performer can "show off" his technique by performing brilliantly a scale or arpeggio *passage.*

passepied (pahss-PYAY, French, "pass foot"). A spirited, gay, French dance, with the feeling of a quick minuet, in 3/8 or 6/8 time. *Passepieds* were fashionable in the 17th-century French court.

passing notes. Tones which harmonically do not belong to the chords they are next to, but which act as a bridge to connect one chord to another chord. There are two kinds of passing tones, accented and unaccented.

pastoral or **pastorale.** 1. Instrumental or vocal music which imitates country sounds and attempts to convey a country air and rural scenes. A famous example is Beethoven's *Pastoral Symphony,* published in 1809. 2. Music in 6/8 time which imitates the sound of the shepherd's bagpipe. 3. A story form, usually about country life, set to music, popular in Europe in the 15th to 18th centuries, which was a forerunner of the opera.

patriotic airs or **songs.** Songs which tell of the history or glories of a country. "Yankee Doodle" and "God Bless America" are examples.

patron. In music, a person who gives money to composers or musicians to help them continue their studies and work. Also, a person who contributes to the cost of running a musical organization, such as an orchestra or opera company.

pattern. A melody sequence or group of notes repeated over and over again. In a *rhythmic pattern* the same rhythm is repeated.

patter song. A fast, funny song in which a string of words is uttered as rapidly as possible. It adds to the comic effect if the string is nonsensical. There are many delightful examples of *patter songs* in the light operas of Gilbert and Sullivan.

pause. A sign (𝄐) to wait or to hold a note. Also known as a fermata.

pavane (pah-VAHN). A slow, dignified dance in 4/4 time of Spanish or Italian origin introduced to instrumental music in the 16th century. Many scholars believe that the *pavane* takes its name from the Spanish and Italian words meaning "peacock." The implication is that the dance reminds one of the stately strut of the peacock displaying his beautiful feathers. Like many other early dances, the *pavane* was sung as well as danced. A modern illustration is Ravel's "Pavane for a Dead Princess," originally written for piano.

pedal. The action in musical instruments controlled by the feet. On the piano, *pedals* are the three levers attached to metal rods at the bottom of the instrument. (*See* **damper pedal, soft pedal, sostenuto pedal.**) On a pipe organ, the *pedals* comprise the wooden keyboard played by the feet. On a reed organ they are the treadles, which when pressed alternately, force air into the instrument. The harp has seven *pedals* which, when pressed, alter the pitch by raising it a half tone. The kettledrum's *pedal* also controls its pitch. (Illus. p. xvi)

pedal point. A long note, usually in the bass, held against changing harmonies in the other voices. In a true *pedal point,* chords change from harmony to dissonance and back to harmony again, while the original pedal tone is held.

peg. A key-shaped pin of wood or metal that holds the string of a stringed instrument in its socket. The *peg* is tightened for a higher sound, and loosened for a lower sound.

pentatonic scale. A very old five-note scale found in early Chinese, Japanese, Far Eastern and African music, in use long before today's major and minor scales. In the *pentatonic scale* there are no half steps between the notes, and the fourth and seventh degrees of the major scale are missing. Examples: c d f g a or c♯ d♯ f♯ g♯ a♯

percussion choir. Drums, gongs, bells and cymbals—the percussion section of an orchestra.

percussion instrument. The drum, bells, castanets, piano, and any other instrument that has to be struck to make a sound.

perdendosi (per-den-DOE-see, Italian.) Let the music gradually die away. (*abbrev.* perd.)

performer. In music, one who sings, plays an instrument, or dances for the entertainment of others.

pesante (pe-SAHN-te, Italian, "weighing"). Make the music sound heavy, important.

phonetics. The study of pronunciation of words, including the way they are produced by the vocal organs and their effect on the ear.

phrase. A part of a melody. The entire melody may be thought of as a musical sentence; the *phrase* as a part of the sentence. (Illus. p. xvi)

phrase balance. The "question and answer" feeling common to all music. The "question" may be asked by one phrase, and the "answer" given by another phrase.

phrasing. 1. The division of music

into "thoughts" or "sentences." The notes contained in a phrase are usually connected by slurs which are printed over them. 2. Breath control and attention to accent and cadence in singing or playing.

pianissimo (pee-en-ISS-imoe, Italian). Play or sing very softly. (*abbrev.* pp.)

pianist (pee-AN-ist, Italian). A person who plays the piano.

piano (pee-AN-oe, Italian). 1. Play or sing softly. (*abbrev.* p.) 2. A stringed percussion keyboard instrument developed around 1710 by B. Cristafori of Florence, Italy. *Piano* is an abbreviation of the word "pianoforte," which in a sense expresses the genius of this instrument. *Piano* is the Italian word for "soft"; forte, for "loud." Thus, "pianoforte" describes an instrument which can be played both softly and loudly. This could not be done with its forebears, such as virginals and harpsichords. The pianoforte, in this respect, owed its versatility to two mechanical features: a hammer that

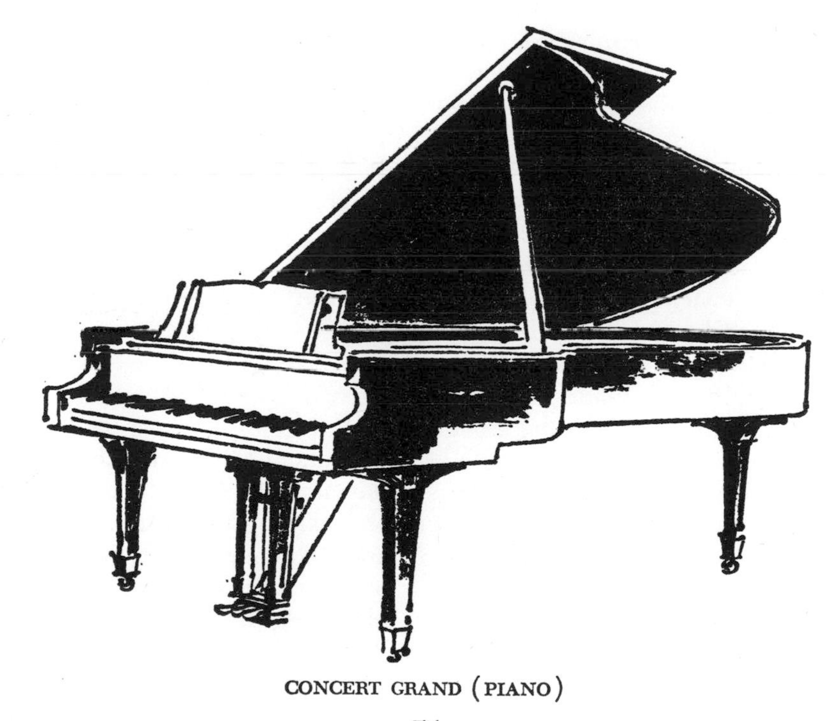

CONCERT GRAND (PIANO)

struck a string returned immediately to its rest position leaving the string to vibrate; and dampers which fell upon the string and suppressed the vibration. The performer could make use of these devices and thereby play the instrument *piano* or forte. The modern piano has eighty-eight ivory or plastic-covered keys (fifty-two white and thirty-six black). Each key moves a felt-covered wooden hammer which strikes the metal strings inside the instrument. This makes them vibrate against a wooden sounding board. Length and thickness of the strings determine the pitch of the tones. Most *pianos* have three pedals—the damper (sometimes called the loud) pedal, the sostenuto pedal, and the soft pedal—which enable the player to control the volume and fullness of the music (*See* **damper pedal, sostenuto pedal, soft pedal**). A *grand piano* for the home is shaped like a harp lying on its side. It is made in about six different sizes, ranging from 5 feet to 6 feet 4 inches in length. A *concert grand piano* for the stage is shaped like the *grand piano,* but is much longer, stretching out to 10 feet. In an *upright piano* (a spinet, console, or studio upright) the strings and sounding board are arranged vertically instead of horizontally.

pianoforte. *See* **piano.**

pianola (pee-ah NOE-lah). A mechanical player piano which had many predecessors patented by the American, E. S. Votey, in 1897. Pierced paper rolls inserted in the upper middle part of the *pianola* move over a slotted metal cylinder. Air, pumped through the cylinder by foot pedals, causes piano hammers to strike the strings, producing sound.

PIANOLA

piano tuner. A person who adjusts the pitch of a piano by tightening or loosening its strings. He uses a small tool to twist the tuning pins which hold the strings in place, and a tuning fork to test their pitch.

piatti (pee-AH-tee, Italian). Cymbals.

pibroch (PEE-brahk). Scottish music written for the bagpipe.

piccolo (PIK-oe-loe, Italian, "little"). A woodwind instrument, 12½ inches long, which looks like a

PICCOLO

small flute. Pitched an octave higher than the flute, the *piccolo* has the highest sound of any woodwind in an orchestra. There is one *piccolo* in a full symphony orchestra.

pick. A small piece of metal or other hard material used to pluck the strings of a ukulele.

pipe. A simple wind instrument consisting of a hollow tube, with holes through which air is blown to produce sound. One of the earliest examples is the shepherd's *pipe.*

pitch. The sound of a musical tone, either high or low. The sound of one note in a scale compared to the other notes in the scale. *Pitch* of a tone depends upon the frequency of air vibrations which produce it. *See* **absolute pitch, perfect pitch.**

piu (pyoo, Italian). More. Example: *Più lento* means "more slowly."

piu lento (pyoo LEN-toe, Italian). Play or sing slowly.

pizzicato (pitz-zi-KAH-toe, Italian). The effect produced by plucking the strings of a stringed instrument with the fingers. (*abbrev.* pizz.)

placido (pla-SEE-doe, Latin). Play gently and calmly.

plainsong. The music of the early Roman Catholic church services. *See* **Gregorian chant.**

player piano. *See* **pianola.**

plectrum. A small thin piece of metal, ivory, or bone used to pluck the strings of a mandolin, guitar, or lute.

plucking. Twanging a string to make a quick, sharp sound. *See* **pizzicato.**

poco (POE-koe, Italian). A little. Example: *Poco meno mosso* means "a little less rapidly."

poco a poco (POE-koe ah POE-koe, Italian). Little by little.

poco meno mosso (POE-koe MEN-oe MOE-soe, Italian). Play or sing with less movement, or more slowly.

poco piu moto (POE-koe pyoo MOE-toe, Italian). Play a little more quickly.

poco ritenuto (POE-koe ree-te-NOO-toe, Italian). Hold or wait a little.

polka (POLE-kah). A dance in 2/4 time that came from Bohemia (the old name for Czechoslovakia). Usually danced by couples. The word *polka* means "half" and describes the short, quick half steps of the dance. After 1835, the *polka* gradually spread to other countries and by the end of the 19th century had become a tremendously popular social dance.

POLKA

polka mazurka (POLE-kah mah-ZUR-kah). A fast polka in 3/4 time.

polonaise (POLE-ah-naize). A proud, commanding ballroom dance in 3/4 time thought to have first been used in the 16th century at the election of a Polish king. In later centuries the stately music of the *polonaise* was played for the king and his court as they promenaded around the ballroom. In the 19th century, Chopin wrote *polonaises* expressing the patriotism and heroism of the Polish people.

polyphony. Literally, "many-sound" or "many-voice" music. Music containing two or more separate melodic lines which are sounded at the same time and blend harmonically with each other. One might think of the independent melodies as two persons in a dance winding in and out, forming figures, at times arm in arm, and then going their separate ways. Polyphonic music, although many centuries old, retains its vitality to this day and is written by modern composers.

polytonality. Music written in two different keys at the same time. A familiar example is Stravinsky's ballet, *Petrushka.*

"pop" concert. An orchestral performance, frequently played out of doors for large audiences, the program ranging from some of the best-known symphonies to light and tuneful compositions. Many cities have *pop* orchestras to give these concerts. One of the most famous is the Boston *Pops* Orchestra founded by Arthur Fiedler.

portamento (por-tah-MEN-toe, Italian). 1. In singing, to let a sound glide smoothly and rapidly from one note to another. 2. A glissando on the violin and trombone. 3. In piano playing, a half-staccato. To quote a famous teacher, "It's as if you were trying to play legato with one finger." (*abbrev.* port.)

position. 1. In playing a stringed instrument, the four fingers of the left hand press down at different sets of places on the strings. Each of these places is called a *position.* They are numbered *first position, second position,* and so forth. 2. In trombone playing, the placing of the slide, at varying points.

potpourri (poe-poor-REE, French, "rotten pot"). A mixture of tunes thrown together, with only slight links between them. A *potpourri* aims at nothing more than pleasant musical entertainment.

practice. In music, to repeat a song or composition until it is as perfect as one can make it. Learning music is like learning a part in a play. First, one reads it through to get the meaning, and the "flow"; then one takes a section at a time and repeats it until the whole piece is mastered.

preciso (pre-CHEE-soe, Italian). Play exactly keeping the rhythm very definite.

prelude (PREL-yood). 1. The beginning of, or introduction to, a piece of music. Example: Bach's "Preludes and Fugues." 2. A short composition in one movement. Examples: Chopin's twenty-four "Preludes for the Piano." 3. A short orchestral operatic overture, which previews the music to follow. Example: Wagner's "Die Meistersinger."

première (pre-MYAIR, French). In music, the first performance of a new composition.

prestissimo (pres-TISS-i-moe, Italian). Play very quickly.

presto (PRES-toe, Italian). Quickly.

prima donna (PRIM-ah DON-nah, Italian). The leading lady in an opera. Diva.

primitive dance. The dance is one of the earliest forms of tribal expression. The name *primitive dance* describes loosely an art form which expresses the life, work, religion, magical beliefs, fears, and so on, of a group of primitive people. The American Indians, the ancient Egyptians, and the various tribes of Africa have all had their dances. The war dance of the American Indians is a good example.

primo (PREE-moe, Italian, "first"). 1. In a duet, the upper part. (The lower part is called "secundo.") 2. A direction to go back to the original time of singing or playing. Example: *Tempo primo.* 3. The first of two or more singers or players, the *violino primo,* for example, is the first violin of a string quartet, or the entire first violin section of an orchestra. A passage of a violin score marked *primo* is to be played by the first violin.

processional. A stately and dignified hymn sung in a church while the choir and clergy enter.

prodigy. In music, a child who very early in life shows great talent and ability on a musical instrument. Even when he is very young, he excites wonder among adults and can play as well as a grown-up artist. However, many fine musicians have taken many years to become as expert as they are.

professional musician. A person who earns his living by writing, arranging, teaching, or performing music.

program music. Sometimes called descriptive music. Music that tells a story, describes a scene, or paints a musical picture. Beethoven's *Pastoral Symphony,* Debussy's *Reflections in the Water,* and Dukas' *Sorcerer's Apprentice* are excellent examples.

progression. A succession of tones or chords, one after the other. *Melodic progressions* move forward from tone to tone. *Harmonic progressions* move forward from chord to chord.

progressive jazz. A kind of modern jazz music which developed from bebop. Sometimes called the "chamber music" of jazz, it is music for listening rather than dancing. Dave Brubeck is a well known *progressive jazz* pianist.

psalms (sahmz). A religious song of praise for chorus or solo voice, an ancestor of the chorale and the hymn. The word *psalm* especially applies to verses from the Old Testament set to music for both Jewish and Christian services.

psalmist (SAHM-ist). 1. A composer of psalms. 2. In the 16th century, a cantor (singer) in the Hebrew synagogue.

psalter (SAHL-ter). The Book of Psalms, translated into English, French, and other languages and arranged for singing by the church congregation. In the 15th century, many reformed churches adopted the *psalter* in place of psalms and often based their hymns on the New rather than the Old Testament.

psaltery. A medieval stringed instrument known to the Jews as a "kinnor" and to the Arabs as a "kanun." The *psaltery* was somewhat like a small dulcimer or a zither, and was plucked with a plectrum. The Austrian zither is a modern version of the *psaltery.*

pulse. The feeling of strong and weak beats in music. For example, a measure in 3/4 time would have the following *pulse:* strong, weak, weak. In 4/4 time, the pulse would be: strong, weak, weak, weak.

Q

quadrille. The real ancestor of the American square dance. The *quadrille* was a French court dance which spread to England and Germany in the early 19th century. It was performed by two to four couples moving in a square. It consisted of five move-

QUADRILLE

ments either in 6/8 or 2/4 time and was danced to the popular music of the day.

quadruplet. A group of four notes played in the same amount of time in which only three notes are played such as 4 eighth notes played in the time of 3 eighth notes.

quarter note. A black note with a stem attached equal in value to one quarter of a whole note. In quarter time a *quarter note* gets one beat.

quarter rest. A sign instructing the performer to pause for a period equal in time to the length of one quarter note. *See* **notes and rests.**

quarter time. The time indicated when a 4 is the bottom number of the meter signature. Example: 2/4, 3/4, 4/4. The 4 represents a quarter note, which gets one beat.

quartet. Four people playing instruments or singing or dancing together.

quasi (KWAH-see, Italian). As if, almost. For example, *quasi vivace* means almost lively.

quickstep. 1. A lively military march in 6/8 or 2/4 time popular about 1811. 2. A lively fox trot.

quintet. Five people playing instruments, singing, or dancing together.

quinton. A French violin with five strings used in the 18th century.

quintuplet. A group of five notes played in the same amount of time in which only four notes are played, such as 5 eighth notes to be played in the time of 4 eighth notes.

quodlibet. An assortment of different folk tunes. There are two types of *quodlibets:* 1. An arrangement in which the tunes follow each other in rapid succession. 2. An arrangement in which several tunes are performed at the same time. An example is the last of Bach's *Goldberg Variations* which contains well-known tunes of the day.

R

ragtime. Highly syncopated popular music, primarily for the piano, which became popular at the end of the last century. Because of its syncopated rhythm it was first called "ragged music."

railroad songs. Folk songs which had their beginnings in the 19th century among the men who worked on the railroads. Some were sung to the rhythms of the men chopping and swinging with their axes. Others, which told stories of famous railroad men of the past, were sung around the campfire or in the bunkhouse. "Drill Ye Tarriers Drill" was a *railroad song* sung by unskilled Irish laborers (called "tarriers") as they removed loosened rock. "Casey Jones" is the most famous American *railroad song.*

RAILROAD SONG

rallentando (rahl-en-TAHN-doe, Italian). Go slower and slower. (*abbrev.* rall.)

range. The distance between the highest and lowest tones a voice or instrument is able to play.

rapido (RA-pee-doe, Italian). Play or sing a passage very quickly.

rasch (rahsh, German). Play or sing quickly.

realistic music. A type of program music written to imitate actual, nonmusical sounds, such as a train whistle or street traffic.

rebec. One of the earliest forms of the violin. Shaped like a half pear, it had three gut strings and was played with a bow. The *rebec*

REBEC

was adapted from the Arabian rebab and was used in Europe in the 16th century.

recapitulation. A final section towards the end of the first movement in sonata form which returns to the themes of the opening section (called the "exposition"). The repeated themes of the *recapitulation* are usually in the tonic key. *See* **sonata form.**

recessional. The hymn sung at the close of a religious service.

recital. A performance of songs or instrumental music by one or two soloists (as opposed to a concert which is a performance by a group of performers). Many people think of Franz Liszt as the first truly great artist to give a *recital.*

recitative (re-ci-tah-TEEV, Italian). Vocal music which sounds as much like dramatic speech as it does like singing. The tone and rhythm of a *recitative* are extremely important; the melody much less so. The form developed early in the 17th century and was used in operas, and in oratorios, cantatas, and other types of church music. Mozart's opera, *Don Giovanni,* first performed in 1787, has passages of *recitative.*

recorder. A woodwind instrument of the flute family, but much easier to play than the flute. The

RECORDER

player blows into a whistle-type mouthpiece and produces sweet, gentle tones by fingering a row of eight holes. *Recorders* are made in four sizes: soprano, alto, tenor, and bass.

reed. 1. A thin tongue of cane used as a mouthpiece or part of a mouthpiece on many wind instruments. The vibration of the *reed* helps to produce the characteristic woodwind sound. A *single-reed* instrument (such as a clarinet or a saxophone) is so called because it has a single *reed* fastened to its mouthpiece. The mouthpiece of a *double-reed* instrument (such as an oboe, bassoon, or English horn) consists of two *reeds* bound together. 2. A thin metal tongue that beats against the opening of an organ pipe. Its action is very similar to that of the *clarinet reed.*

reed stops. The knobs or lever controls which regulate the reed pipes on an organ. The reed pipe section is divided into the chorus, semichorus, and solo reeds.

reel. A lively, gay, country-dance that originated in northern Europe, was later performed in Scotland and Ireland, and eventually came to Colonial America where it became known as the *Virginia reel.* It is usually danced by two or more couples facing each other and forming a figure eight with their steps.

refrain. The main part—or chorus—of a song, hymn, or ballad which is repeated after each verse or stanza is sung.

register. 1. A set of pipes in an organ controlled by one stop. 2. A range of the voice. In singing the *head register* makes higher sounds; the *chest register,* lower sounds. 3. A portion of an instrument's total sound range, such as the *high register* of the trombone, the *low register* of the bassoon, and so forth.

registration. The skill and ability with which an organ player uses organ registers. He must know how to choose and combine the stops to produce the various sounds.

relative minor scale. A ladder of tones in which the third degree is a half step lower than the third degree of a major scale. Each major scale has three relative minors: the natural, the harmonic (which is the most commonly used), and the melodic. These scales are sometimes thought of as first cousins (or "relatives") of their major scales because they have the same "family name" or key signature. The *relative minor scale* always begins on the sixth degree of the relative major. One can find it easily by counting down one and a half steps from the first note of the major scale. For example, the relative minor of G major is e minor (e being one and a half steps below G).

The minor scales conform to the following patterns: *natural* 6 7 8 2 3 4 5 6; *harmonic* 6 7 8 2 3 4 ♯5 6; *melodic* 6 7 8 2 3 ♯4 ♯5 6. (Descending, the melodic scale is like the natural scale, 6 5 4 3 2 1 7 6.)

repeat. Play a piece, or part of a piece, again. (Illus. p. xvi)

repertoire (re-per-TWAHR, French). A group of songs, dances, or musical compositions which the performer has prepared to present before an audience.

Requiem. 1. In the Roman Catholic church, a Mass sung in memory of someone who has died. 2. A musical setting, usually for chorus, and often also for orchestra, of portions of this Mass. Many *Requiems,* such as those by Verdi and Berlioz, are considered too dramatic to be used in the church. The Brahms *Requiem* is not a setting of the Catholic service, but an oratorio, using passages from the German translation of the New Testament.

rest. A sign directing a performer to allow a period of silence. There are many kinds of *rests,* each one equal in time value to a corresponding note. A quarter *rest,* for example, instructs the performer to pause for a period equal to the time value of a quarter note. *See* **notes and rests.**

restez (RES-tay, French, "stay"). In bow instrument playing, play in the same position (first, third, fifth position), for example, until a change is indicated.

reveille (REV-il-lee, French). The "time to get up" song played by the bugler in the army or at a camp.

rhapsody. An excited, sometimes gay, instrumental composition in free form developed in the 19th and 20th centuries. A *rhapsody* often borrows its melodies from folk music and has a patriotic or national flavor. Johannes Brahms used this form in his *rhapsodies* for the piano and Franz Liszt wrote twenty Hungarian *rhapsodies* based on European gypsy tunes. George Gershwin's *Rhapsody in Blue* is a good modern example of a composer letting his imagination run free using jazz melodies.

rhythm. 1. The arrangement of music so that it has a constant beat or pulse. *Metrical rhythm* refers to the various patterns of accent that occur in standard meters: 2/4 (strong, weak); 3/4 (strong, weak, weak); 4/4 (strong, weak, weak, weak).

riff. In jazz, a repeated, improvised phrase, usually two to four bars long.

r.h. An abbreviation for the "right hand." Used to indicate that the passage is to be played with the right hand.

rigaudon (REE-goe-don, French).

An early French dance in 2/4 or 4/4 time performed with a very lively jumping step. The *rigaudon* was introduced to the French operatic ballet in the 17th century.

rigore (ri-GOR-e, Italian). Play or sing in strict time.

ripetizione (re-pe-ti-tzi-OE-ne, Italian). Repeat.

risoluto (ri-zo-LOO-toe, Italian). Perform in a decisive way as though the music were moving forcefully toward a goal.

ritardando (ri-tar-DAN-doe, Italian). Slowing down. (*abbrev.* ritard.)

ritardato senza (ri-tar-DAH-toe SEN-zah, Italian). Keep playing without slowing down.

ritardo (ri-TAR-doe, Italian). Gradually slow down. (*abbrev.* ritard.)

ritenuto (ri-te-NOO-toe, Italian). Hold back, play in slower time.

robusto (roe-BOOS-toe, Italian). Play or sing in a firm, bold way.

rock and roll. A type of jazz music with a strongly accented beat. There are a number of *rock-and-roll* styles; one of the most common has a 12/8 rhythm. *Rock and roll* can be traced back to boogie-woogie.

ROCK AND ROLL

roll. A trill on the snare, kettle, or bass drums.

romance. A short instrumental or vocal composition often with a sentimental, dreamlike quality. Originally the *romance* was a ballad sung by minstrels.

romantic school. A group of 19th-century composers who in general put more emphasis on individual feeling and expression in music than on strict form. Melody became more important, harmony became freer, rhythms were used with more daring, and new forms, such as the symphonic poem, were used. Liszt, Chopin, Mendelssohn, Brahms, and Schumann were composers of the *romantic school.*

romanza (roe-MAHN-zah, Italian). A romance.

rondo (Italian). An instrumental or vocal form very popular in the late 18th and early 19th centuries. The principal theme is consistently repeated throughout the piece. The outline of a *rondo* is best illustrated by the letter sequence A B A C A in which A is the principal theme, B the second theme, C the third theme. Mozart and Beethoven both wrote *rondos* for the piano. Other composers have used the form in sonatas, string quartets, concertos, and symphonies.

root. The basic note upon which a chord is built. A chord is named for its *root*. For example, G is the root of the G triad GBD.

rosin (also **resin**). A hard gum that is rubbed on the hair of a bow to help the bow grip the strings and to produce a steady sound.

roulade (roo-LAHD, French). In vocal or instrumental music, a quick-moving group of grace notes that connects one tone to another tone. Used in coloratura arias in some 18th- and 19th-century operas.

round. A simple musical form following the principle of imitation (the repetition of a theme or melody in different parts of a composition). A *round* is made up of three or more parts sung by several people either on the same tone or an octave apart. The first person starts singing the tune, then a few measures later, the second singer begins while the first continues the song. Again after a few measures, the third person enters while the others continue to sing. "Three Blind Mice" and "Frère Jacques" are two familiar *rounds. See* **canon.**

roundelay. A circle dance, going back to the 14th century.

rubato (roo-BAH-toe, Italian, "robbed"). A flexibility of tempo in which the time value of certain notes is "robbed" from them and given to other notes in a measure or phrase. This technique is used to give the music a freedom of tempo both in melody and accompaniment. Slowing down or speeding up for a *rubato* adds much to the expressiveness of a performance.

rumba (ROOM-bah, Cuban). A Cuban dance of African origin with a lively syncopated beat. It

RUMBA

repeats an eight-measure theme constantly, the beat being more important than the melody. Movements of the body are emphasized much more than those of the feet.

run. A group of notes in scale form played or sung very quickly.

S

saltando (sahl-TAHN-doe, Italian, "leaping"). In string instrument playing, permitting the bow to bounce lightly on the strings.

saltarello (sahl-tah-REL-loe, from the Italian *saltare,* "to jump"). A 16th-century Italian dance, quick and violent in motion. Danced in 6/8 time, it is very much like the tarantella.

samisen. A rectangular-shaped Japanese stringed instrument which looks something like a guitar or a lute. It has three strings tuned in fifths or fourths and is plucked with a plectrum. It is very popular with geisha and street singers.

SAMISEN

sarabande (SAHR-ah-band, French). A slow, stately dance popular in England in the 17th and 18th centuries. It is usually in 3/4 time and follows a rhythm pattern in which the accent is on the second beat. The *sarabande* actually originated as a lively dance popular in 16th-century Spain.

saxophone. Although made of metal, the *saxophone* is considered a member of the woodwind family. It combines the single-reed mouthpiece of the clarinet with the conical bore of the oboe. The instrument was invented by Adolphe Sax in 1846 and is one of the youngest members of the woodwind family. It has become very popular with military and jazz bands and is sometimes in-

SAXOPHONE

cluded in an orchestra. *Saxophones* come in a variety of sizes and have a range of almost three octaves.

scale (from the Italian *scala,* "ladder"). A ladder or series of tones, going up or down, separated by whole or half steps. The most widely used *scales* are: *major, minor, chromatic, pentatonic,* and *whole tone.* See separate entries on each of these *scales.*

scat singing. A kind of singing often used in jazz in which the performer sings a rapid string of nonsense syllables instead of words.

scherzando (scare-ZAHN-doe, Italian). Play or sing in a humorous, bouncy way. (*abbrev.* scherz.)

scherzo (SCARE-tso, Italian, "joke"). 1. A lively, humorous piece. 2. The third movement of a symphony, string quartet, or sonata. Beethoven and Bruckner both included *scherzos* in many of their compositions.

schottische (SHOT-eesh, German-Scottish). A lively round dance in 2/4 time much like the polka, but a little slower. In 19th-century England, the *schottische* was known as the "German polka."

score. An arrangement of the instrumental and vocal parts of a musical composition in which each part is written one above the other on a separate staff. An *orchestral* or *full score* is an arrangement of all of the instruments and vocal parts of a symphonic or orchestral work. A *vocal score* contains a full transcription of all vocal parts but the instrument parts are reduced to a piano arrangement.

sea shanty. A sailor's work song, a folk song of the sea. The sailors sang *sea shanties* as they furled the sails or scrubbed the decks

SEA SHANTY

of the old sailing vessels. "Blow the Man Down" is one of the most famous *sea shanties*.

secondo (se-KUN-doe, Italian). The second (or lower) part in a duet.

segno (SEN-yo, Italian). A sign (printed :S:) meaning "repeat." *Al segno* means "to the sign." *Dal segno* means "from the sign." *Dal segno al fine* means "go back to the sign and play or sing to the end (or *fine*) of the piece."

segue (SEH-goo-eh, Italian). A direction to continue repeating a previous pattern of chords or notes or to continue to the next movement without a break.

seguidilla (se-gwe-DEE-ya, Spanish). A Spanish dance in 3/4 or 3/8 time performed to an accompaniment of guitars and castanets. There are three kinds of *seguidillas*, each of which has different music: *manchegas*, lively and gay; *boleros*, more stately; and *gitanas*, very slow and dreamlike.

semitone. A half step. On the piano, the interval between the white keys b and c, or e and f; or between a white key and an adjacent black key such as g and g♯, or d and d♭.

semplice (sem-PLEE-chay, Italian). Play very simply—in a plain way.

sempre (SEM-pray, Italian). Always. For example, *sempre legato* means "play the music always (or steadily) legato."

senza (SEN-zah, Italian). Without. For example, *senza pedale* means "without pedal."

senza repetitione (SEN-zah re-pe-ti-tsi-OE-ne, Italian). Play without repeating.

septet. Music for seven voices or instruments. Beethoven wrote a *septet* for violin, viola, cello, double bass, horn, clarinet, and bassoon.

sequence. A phrase which is repeated with the same rhythm and the same melody but played on a different pitch level.

serenade. A short evening song. Originally the love song of a suitor sung beneath his lady's window. Later a *serenade* was a set of movements for small (or chamber) orchestras very much like the *divertimenti* of the 18th century. *Serenades* were often written for evening performances. Mozart's "Eine Kleine Nachtmusik" is an example of this form.

serene. Play or sing calmly, gently.

serioso (seer-ee-OE-soe, Italian). Play or sing gravely, in a serious way.

sextet. Music for six voices or instruments, Beethoven's "Wind-Sextet" was written for two clarinets, two bassoons, and two horns. Brahms' "String Sextet" was written for two violins, two violas, and two celli.

sforzando (sfor-TZAHN-doe, Italian, "forcing"). An accent sign. Play or sing the notes it marks with a strong, sudden accent. (*abbrev.* sf. or sfz.)

sharp. A sign meaning to raise a tone one half step. *See* **accidentals.** (Illus. p. xvi)

shofar (SHOW-far). A ram's horn dating back to ancient Hebrew biblical times, originally used in battle or at sacred festivals.

SHOFAR

Sounded in the synagogue to celebrate the arrival of the Jewish New Year, and on the Day of Atonement. The *shofar* makes two primitive sounds a fifth apart in pitch.

shout song. Songs which were sung at religious camp meetings or

SHOUT SONG

revivals. *Shout songs* were part song, part dance; they were accompanied by great religious excitement, hand clapping and stamping of the feet. "Joshua Fit de Battle of Jericho" was a *shout song* sung by southern Negroes during the last century.

siciliana (see-cheel-YAN-ah, Italian). An Italian dance in 6/8 time, graceful and slow in movement, quite similar to the pastorale. Originally the *siciliana* was a dance performed by Sicilian peasants. Seventeenth- and 18-century composers used the form for both instrumental and vocal music.

sight reading. The ability to play or sing music upon seeing the printed score for the first time. A good sight reader immediately notes the key signature of a piece, its melody direction and rhythms, and any special difficulties it presents. While singing or playing an experienced sight reader usually keeps his eye one measure ahead, anticipating the notes to be played or sung.

signature. A sign, placed at the beginning of a composition. *See* **key signature, time signature.**

sinfonietta (sin-fon-NYET-tah, Italian). A small symphony, usually for a chamber orchestra.

singing. The art of performing vocal music.

sistrum. An ancient Egyptian instrument, used by the worshippers of the goddess Isis. The

SISTRUM

sistrum was shaped like a rattle. It had a handle and an oval-shaped metal frame to which metal rods were loosely attached. These rods jingled when the player shook the instrument.

sixteenth note. A black note with two flags. In quarter time, four *sixteenth notes* get one count. *See* **notes and rests.**

sixteenth rest. A symbol indicating a period of silence equal to the time value of a sixteenth note. *See* **notes and rests.**

slargando (slar-GAHN-doe, Italian). Relax and slow down.

slentando (slen-TAHN-doe, Italian). Same as *slargando.*

slur. A curved line drawn over or under a group of two or more notes indicating that the notes within the curve should be played or sung smoothly. In music for stringed instruments, all notes under a *slur* are to be played on one bow stroke. In music for wind instruments, only the first of a group of slurred notes is tongued. The remaining notes are played without a fresh attack and with a steady, flowing tone. No "space" is heard between the slurred notes. (Illus. p. xvi)

smorzando (smor-ZAN-doe, Italian). Let the sound gradually die away. (*abbrev.* smorz.)

snare drum. A percussion instrument, the smallest of the three drums used in a symphony orchestra. It consists of a cylindrical frame covered with tightly stretched pieces of calfskin. Two hoops which bind the heads to the cylinder are connected by metal rods. Across the thinner, bottom head of the drum are stretched strings known as "snares," which

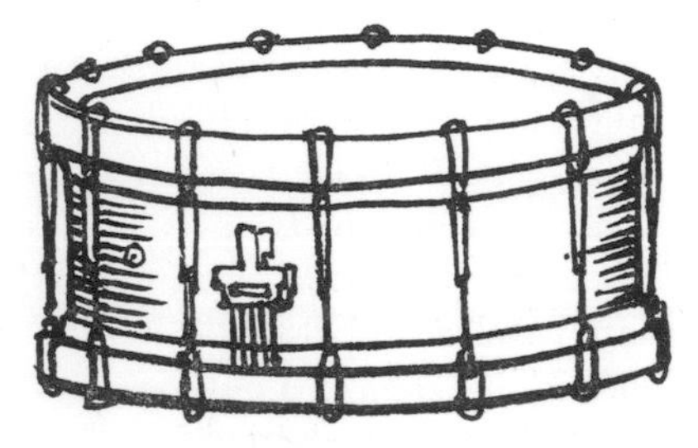

SNARE DRUM

rattle against the calfskin to produce the characteristic *snare drum* sound. The *snare drum* has no definite pitch. It is also called the "small" or "side drum."

soft pedal. The left pedal on the piano which permits the performer to play with a softer tone. The *soft pedal's* movement shifts the keyboard and action to the right so that the hammers strike only one of the two or three strings which produce a particular tone.

solfeggio. Vocal exercises used in ear training and sight singing in which the singer identifies the syllables, *do, re, mi, fa, sol, la, ti, do,* with the degrees of the scale. There are two methods of applying these syllables to the scale degrees: the movable- and fixed-do systems. 1. The fixed do is always C in the C major scale, *re* is always D, *mi* is e, and so on. If a work is in e minor it can also be described as being in "mi minuer (minor)" e being the fixed *mi.* Another word for this system is "solmization." It is said to have been invented by Guido d'Arezzo in the 11th century and was used in France and Italy. 2. Movable *do.* The syllables were used originally as *doh, ray, me, fah, soh, lah, te, doh. Doh* is the first degree of whatever key the composition is in. America and England use the movable-*doh* system which was invented by Sarah Glover in 1812 and developed by John Curwen in 1840. (Both musicians were English.)

solo. Music for one voice or one instrument, with or without accompaniment.

sonata (so-NAH-tah, Italian). A composition in three or four movements written for one or two instruments. Each movement is complete by itself, yet all of the movements are related to one another. Generally, classical *sonatas* follow this pattern: first movement, allegro, in *sonata* form; second movement, slow, usually a theme and variations, or possibly another *sonata* form; third movement, quick and gay, a scherzo or minuet; fourth movement, a fast tempo, often a rondo or in *sonata* form. This movement is called the "finale" and is usually fiery and powerful.

sonata form. One of the most commonly used plans for a movement of a sonata, symphony, quartet, or concerto. It consists of three main sections: 1. The exposition in which the themes of the movement are introduced. A first theme is stated in the tonic or home key; a bridge section modulates to an entirely new key; and a second theme is presented in the new key. 2. A development section in which the composer explores the possibilities of his themes. He may try them out in another key or a different rhythm, or perhaps invert them or change their accompaniment. 3. A recapitulation section in which the two themes of the exposition are repeated. This time the second theme is in the home key, or in a key closely related to it. A coda, or concluding section in the home key, may be added after the recapitulation.

sonatina (so-nah-TEE-na, Italian). A small sonata in two or three very short movements, usually fairly easy to play. Clementi wrote many piano *sonatinas* as instruction pieces for beginning students. However, Ravel and other modern composers have used the form for mature musical compositions.

song. A musical setting of words. The singing of *songs* is the most ancient kind of music making. *See* **art song, folk song.**

song element. A melodious feeling in some music that makes it sound as though it were singing. In instrumental music, songlike passages are sometimes described as "lyric."

soprano (so-PRAH-noe, Italian). 1. The highest female singing voice with a range of from middle C to high A. 2. A young boy's voice with the same range. 3. The word *soprano* is also used to describe some high-ranged instruments. Example: *Soprano saxophone.*

SOPRANO

sostenuto (sos-te-NOO-toe, Italian, "sustained"). 1. Hold the notes a little longer, thus slowing up or holding back the time. 2. Fill the entire beat with sound so that no "spaces" are heard between notes.

sostenuto pedal (sos-te-NOO-toe, Italian). The middle pedal on a piano designed to hold one tone or chord while others are being played. A pianist strikes a key while holding down the *sostenuto pedal* with his foot. This first note will continue sounding while he plays a succession of other notes. (*abbrev.* sost. ped.)

sotto voce (SOT-toe VO-che, Italian, "under the voice"). Perform the music in a soft voice as if in an undertone.

sound. Every time you hear a *sound,* this is what happens: waves (just like ocean waves) are created in the air and these strike your eardrum. The *sounds* are carried to the brain through the eardrum, and you "hear" the noise or music or speech. People can hear *sounds* from an octave below the lowest one on a piano to three octaves above the highest piano note. Animals can hear *sounds* even higher than this. *Sound* waves can be tiny or big. They vibrate anywhere from sixteen times per second to 38,000 times per second. A low number of vibrations causes low tones and a high number of vibrations causes high tones. *See* **acoustics.**

sound board. A thin sheet of wood which acts as a resonator, catching sound waves and throwing them back to give music a full, beautiful tone. Stringed instruments, pianos, and organs all have *sound boards.* They must be open to the air to allow the strings to vibrate fully. If you "close the window" on a *sound board*—by muting a violin or closing the harp on a grand piano, for example—the sound becomes softer because the *sound board* is not as free to vibrate the air as before.

sound hole. The opening in the middle of the belly of a stringed instrument which helps to increase the richness and fullness of the instrument's tone. All stringed instruments except those of the harp type have *sound holes.* On the members of the violin family they are sometimes known as "f holes."

sousaphone. A brass instrument first made in the late 19th century, named after the famous band conductor, John Philip Sousa. It is a brother of the bass tuba, which is the lowest of the brass instruments in the orchestra. The *sousaphone* has a wide flaring bell. It is big enough so that the player is able to slip through the curve of its tube and rest the instrument on his shoulders.

SOUSAPHONE

spiccato (spi-COT-toe, Italian). Play with a springing bow making the sounds rapid and clear.

spinet. 1. An early keyboard instrument similar to the harpsichord. 2. Today, a small upright piano

SPINET (PIANO)

designed for homes where space is limited.

spirito (SPIR-i-to, Italian). Play with fire and excitement. (Sometimes written *con spirito.*)

spiritoso (spir-i-TOE-so, Italian). Play briskly, as if you were taking a good walk in the cold air. (*abbrev.* spir.)

spiritual. A religious folk song created by American Negro slaves, telling of their troubles and their yearnings for a better life. After the Civil War, *spirituals* were written down for the first time. The first printed collection, called *Slave Songs of the United States,* was published in 1867.

springing bow. A violinist plays with a *springing bow* when he bounces his bow on the strings and then lets it rebound and bounce once more.

square dance. In the United States a type of folk dance which developed as pioneers migrated into different sections of the country. The *Eastern square dance* is a descendant of the European quadrille. The *Western square dance* developed from the Mexican and old Spanish-California quadrilles. A *square dance* is performed by two or more couples facing each other and moving in a square. Usually stringed instruments play a spirited accompaniment while a "caller" sings out instructions to the dancers. Although *square dances* originated in farm areas they have spread into every type

SQUARE DANCE

of community and are tremendously popular with all age groups.

staccato (sta-COT-toe, Italian). Play or sing each note in a quick, detached manner. *Staccato* is indicated by a dot or pointed dash printed over or under a note. (*abbrev.* stacc.) (Illus. p. xvi)

staff. The lines and spaces on which notes are written. A *treble staff* is a five-line and four-space *staff* on which the treble clef is placed. It is used to print music for voices or instruments of medium or high range such as soprano, flute, or violin. A *bass staff* is a five-line and four-space *staff* on which the bass clef is placed. It is used to print music for voices or instruments of low range, such as a bass voice, a cello or a tuba. A *grand staff* contains eleven lines and ten spaces. The top five lines are used for treble-clef music, the center line represents middle C, the bottom five lines are used for bass-clef music.

stem. The "leg" part of a note. A *stem* running upward is placed on the right side of the note head; running downward, on the left side. See **notes and rests.**

step. Same as *whole step.* A melodic progression from one degree on the staff to the next, that is from line to space or space to line. (Exceptions are E to F and B to C.) See **whole step.**

Stimme (SHTIM-me, German). Voice.

stop. 1. On the organ, the handle or knob which controls the flow of air into the various rows of pipes. By pulling out the various *stops,* the organist can vary the sound of the organ, making it full or thin, or producing tones which imitate the sounds of instruments such as the oboe, flute, and trumpet. 2. The rows of organ pipes connected with the various *stops* described above. 3. In string playing, the act of pressing the tips of the left-hand fingers on a string to shorten its vibrating length. Double stopping means stopping two or more notes at the same time.

stretto (STRET-toe, Italian, "close," "narrow"). 1. In a fugue, bringing the different entries of the theme closer together (that is, with a shorter time interval between them) so that they overlap. 2. A closing passage played more quickly for dramatic effect. Another word for accelerando.

string. The long pieces of wire or gut which produce sound on stringed instruments when bowed, plucked, or hit. (Such instruments include all members of the violin family, the harp, piano, zither, guitar, and so forth.) Tightening a *string* shortens it and raises its pitch. Loosening a *string* makes it longer and lowers its pitch.

string choir. The string family in a symphony orchestra: the violin, viola, cello, and double bass.

string quartet. 1. Music written for four stringed instruments: two violins, viola and cello. A *string quartet* is usually in four movements which correspond to the movements of the classical sonata. Haydn was one of the important developers of this form. 2. The four musicians who play such music together.

string quintet. 1. Music written for a combination of five stringed instruments. The combinations may vary. A *string quintet* might include two violins, two violas, and a cello; or perhaps two violins, one viola, and two celli. 2. The five musicians who play such music together.

stringed instruments. Instruments in which sounds are produced by plucking, touching, and bowing the strings.

stringendo (strin-GEN-do, Italian, "tightening"). Gradually quicken. (*abbrev.* string.)

strings. A nickname for all the stringed instruments in the orchestra.

sub dominant. The fourth tone in the major or minor scale.

sub dominant chord. A chord starting on the fourth tone in a major or minor scale.

subito (SOO-bee-toe, Italian). Suddenly, quickly. For example, *subito piano* means "make the sound suddenly soft."

suspension. Holding back one or more notes of a chord while the remaining notes move on to a succeeding chord. This usually produces a dissonance which is changed again into a harmonic sound. A good example of a *suspension* is the effect created when one member of a group of singers holds a note of a chord while the other singers proceed to another chord.

swing. Popular dance music played smoothly and with a steady beat. It originated in the 1930's, and is usually played by large dance bands.

symphonic poem. Also known as a "tone poem." A type of orchestral program music which depicts a scene, tells a story, or expresses a mood or a poetic idea. Franz Liszt was the originator of the *symphonic poem.* Bedřich Smetana, a Czech composer, also used the form. Between 1874 and 1879, he wrote a group of six *symphonic poems* entitled *My Country,* the favorite one being the second, "The Moldau," which describes the beautiful scenery surrounding the river Moldau.

symphony. A composition in three or four movements for a full orchestra. Modeled after the Italian overture and written in its present-day form since 1750, the *symphony* is often identical in form to the classical sonata or string quartet. Thus, the first movement is usually an allegro in sonata form. The second movement is usually a slow song form, a theme and variations, or another sonata form played slowly. The third movement is a minuet or scherzo. The fourth and final movement is often in rondo or sonata form. Haydn was one of the first composers of *symphonies.* *See* **sonata.**

symphony orchestra. A group of 90 to 110 musicians playing serious music together under the leadership of a conductor. They are divided into four sections: strings, woodwinds, brasses, and percussion instruments. See **orchestra.**

syncopation. A rhythmic pattern created by shifting the regular accent, which is usually on the first beat of a measure, to the second, third, or fourth beats. The accent may also be shifted to a half beat, or, in fact, anywhere in the measure the composer chooses to place it. In other words, the rhythm accents the unnatural—or weak—beat in the music. Among the modern composers who have often used *syncopation* in their music are Bela Bartok, Igor Stravinsky, and Leonard Bernstein. Much modern jazz uses *syncopation* to heighten the rhythmic effect.

T

tambourine (tam-bur-EEN). A percussion instrument consisting of a wooden hoop with a skin stretched over the top and small metal discs called "jingles" inserted in slots around the side. It is played in three ways: by

TAMBOURINE

striking it with the knuckles, by rubbing it with the thumb, or by shaking it. All three methods cause the metal discs to vibrate in rhythm with the music. *Tambourines* were first used by ancient Romans and later by traveling entertainers of the Middle Ages. Still later they became important to early Spanish, Portuguese, and gypsy folk music. By the 19th century they had been adopted by military bands, and today they are part of the percussion group in symphony orchestras.

tango. A Latin-American dance that was brought from Argentina to

TANGO

America and Europe in the early part of this century. A *tango* has a slow, strongly marked syncopated rhythm in 3/4 time. Some modern composers have written *tangos* for instrumental suites while others, among them Granados and Albeniz, have written them for the piano.

tanto (TAHN-toe, Italian). Much or so much. For examples, *andante non tanto* means "slowly but not too much so." *Allegro non tanto* means "not too fast."

taps. The "go to sleep" song played by the bulger in the army and in camp. Also played in final farewell at military funerals. Sometimes drums are used in this ceremony. *Taps* originated in the United States Army in 1862.

tarantella (tar-an-TELL-ah). A fast, Italian dance in 6/8 time named after the poisonous tarantula spider. In the 15th century a superstition sprang up which said that a person bitten by this spider could rid himself of the poison by dancing a *tarantella* energetically enough to produce heavy perspiration. Four hundred years later, composers began to write *tarantellas* in which they imitated the music of this fast, wild dance. Mendelssohn's "Tarantella," one of his songs without words, is well known.

tastiera (Tas-tee-AY-ra, Italian). The violin finger board.

tasto (TAS-toe, Italian). 1. A key on a keyboard. 2. A fret on a lute. 3. A stringed instrument's finger board. *Sul tasto* means bowing near the finger board.

technical principles. The laws of technique a musician or dancer must master to become a good performer.

technical studies. Exercises to improve a musician's or dancer's technique—like the exercises an athlete needs to be limber in his sport.

technique (also **technic**). The ease and physical skill with which a performer uses his fingers to play, his voice to sing, or his body to dance. A person who performs difficult music with ease is said to have good *technique.*

tempo (TEM-poh, Italian). The speed or frequency of the basic pulses of the meter of a piece of music. *Tempos* are often indicated on a musical score by Italian words such as adagio, which means "slow" and presto, which means "fast."

tempo di valse (TEM-poh dee vahls, Italian). Play or sing in the time or with the feeling of a waltz.

tempo giusto (TEM-po gi-OOS-toe, Italian). Play or sing in proper, strict time.

tempo mark. A word or direction, written at the upper left-hand corner of a piece, indicating the speed of the music. For example, presto means "very fast"; adagio means "slow."

tempo rubato (TEM-poo roo-BAH-toe, Italian). *See* **rubato.**

tenor. The highest normal range of a man's voice. The word comes from the Latin *tenere,* which means "to hold." Some medieval four-part music was written for three similar voices and a fourth voice which held the long bottom notes. This fourth voice was at first called the "tenere," and later, simply *tenor.* The *tenor* range is from the second B below middle C to the first G above middle C. A countertenor is a man's voice which sings in a high, trained falsetto, above the normal *tenor* range.

tenor clef. The C clef when placed on the fourth line of the staff.

tenuto (te-NOO-toe, Italian). Hold the note or chord for its full value, sometimes even a bit longer.

ternary form. A three-part form consisting of: 1. A first melody or theme in one basic key. This part may be repeated. 2. The second melody or theme in a key closely related to the key of the first section. 3. The return of the first melody or theme and the return of the first key. The *ternary form* pattern is often symbolized "A-B-A."

tetrachord. A succession of four tones, with a half step between the third and fourth tones. A scale consists of two *tetrachords.* In the major scale both *tetrachords* have the same interval arrangement: step, step, half step. In the harmonic (most often used) minor scale, the *tetrachords* are arranged: step, half step, step, step, half step, step and a half, half step.

theme. The subject of a musical composition. A melody or musical idea which the composer may develop or which he may render in different variations. *See* **sonata form** and **variation.**

theorbo (thee-OR-bo). A large bass lute popular two to three hun-

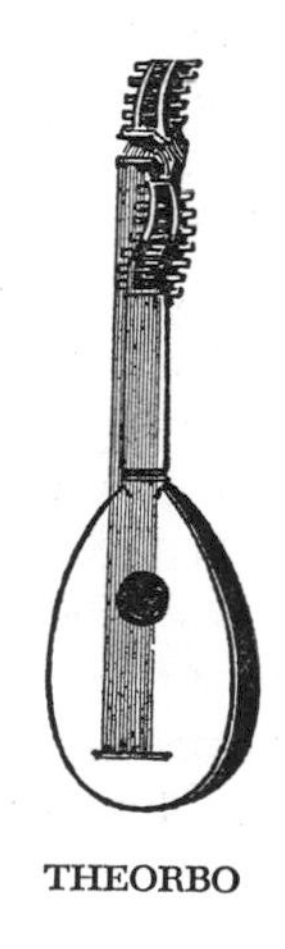

THEORBO

dred years ago. It had a double-peg box and two sets of strings. One set of strings was stopped against the finger board while the other set was played as open-bass strings.

theory. The study of the elements of music, including melody, form, rhythm, harmony, orchestration, and so on. A person who studies music *theory* has two goals: first, to increase his pleasure and understanding as a listener; second, to learn how to use the elements when he writes his own music.

thirty-second note. A very fast black note with three flags attached to its stem. Eight *thirty-second notes* equal one quarter note. *See* **notes and rests.**

thumb string. The banjo string on which the melody is played.

tie. A curve connecting two notes exactly alike in pitch. It is a direction to play the first note and to continue holding it throughout the time value of the second. The second note is not played. This means that the two notes are played as one; their duration is equal to their combined time values. (Illus. p. xvi)

timbre (TAN-br, French). A quality of tone. *See* **tone color.**

time signature. *See* **meter signature.**

timpani (TIM-pan-ee, Italian). The kettle drums. *See* **kettle drums.**

toccata (toc-CAH-tah, Italian). An early keyboard composition, dating from the 16th century, characterized by its quick tempo, many runs, and rapid passages. The word *toccata* comes from an Italian word *toccare,* which means to touch. In a *toccata,* the fingers are supposed to move so quickly they hardly touch the keys.

tonality. The group of chords and harmonies which belong to one key establish *tonality.* For example, if one plays in the key of C and tries to sound all the chords and harmonies belonging to the key of C, a feeling of *tonality* is established.

tone. In music, a sound with a definite pitch (as opposed to a noise which is a confused mixture of pitches).

tone color. Also known as timbre. The characteristic sound of individual instruments or of the different registers of those instruments, or of the voice. *Tone color* results from: 1. The nature of the vibrating part of the instrument, such as a violin string, the column of air in a clarinet, etc. 2. The way the vibration is created, such as by bowing on a string or vibrating the lips when blowing into a trumpet. 3. The shape of the instrument's "resonator," such as the clarinet tube or the harp shape of a grand piano. All these work together to produce the *tone color* of a piece of music.

tone poem. *See* **symphonic poem.**

tonguing. The use of the tongue in wind instrument playing. The tongue serves as a valve to control the flow of air to a vibrating mechanism, such as the reed of a clarinet or saxophone, or the lips of a trumpet or horn player.

tonic. The first note of a scale, which is also the key for which it is named.

tranquillo (trahn-KWEEL-loe, Italian). Play or sing serenely. Make the music quiet and peaceful.

transcribe. To rewrite music for one instrument so that it can be sung or played by another instrument. The original harmony, melody, and rhythm remain unchanged.

transpose. To rewrite music in another key or pitch. Only the pitch is changed; the music remains exactly the same in all other respects.

tre adagio (tray ah-DAH-jeeo, Italian). Play very slowly.

tre corde (tray COR-deh, Italian). In piano playing, use the damper pedal. This moves the dampers away from the strings and lets them vibrate freely. (*abbrev.* T.C.)

treble. The high-range sounds of music. The highest voice part in a choir.

treble clef. The G clef. A sign which indicates that the second line of the staff is to be read as G. Music for the violin, flute, and other high-range instruments is written in the *treble clef.* First used in the 15th century.

tremolo (TRE-mo-loe, Italian). 1. On a violin, the rapid repetition of a single note, produced by sliding the bow back and forth very quickly across one string. 2. On a keyboard the rapid alternation (playing back and forth) of two notes. 3. In singing, a wavering of pitch very much like the vibrato on a stringed instrument.

triads. A chord built in thirds, consisting of a root, a third, and a fifth. There are four kinds of *triads: major, minor, diminished* and *augmented.* A *major triad* contains a major third and a perfect fifth. A *minor triad* contains a minor third and a perfect fifth. A *diminished triad* contains a minor third and a diminished fifth. An *augmented triad* contains a major third and an augmented fifth.

triangle. A percussion instrument consisting of a steel bar bent in the shape of a triangle. The *triangle* is usually played by the drummer in a symphony orchestra. It was first used in the 18th century. When struck with a metal rod it produces a bell-like sound. It has no definite pitch.

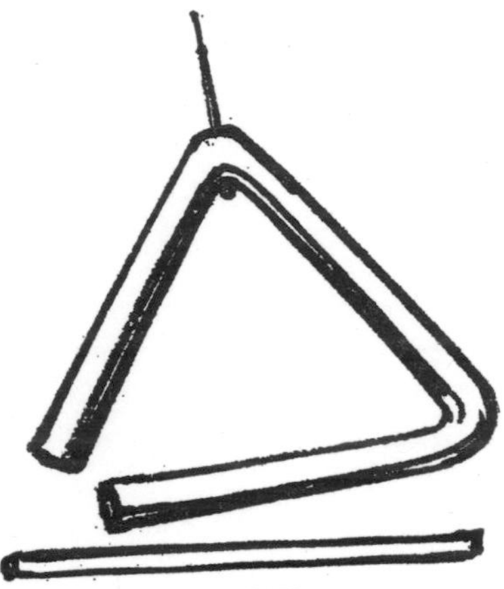

TRIANGLE

trill. Two adjacent racing notes alternating in rapid succession. *Baroque* and sometimes *classical trills* begin on the higher of the two notes. *Romantic trills* usually begin on the lower note.

trio (TREE-oh, Italian). 1. A composition for three instruments, three voices, or three dancers. 2. The second or middle part of a minuet or scherzo after which the first part is repeated.

triple time. A rhythm pattern in which there are three beats to a measure with an accent on the first beat. Examples: 3/4 or 3/8 time.

triplet. A group of three notes played in the same amount of time in which two notes are played in most of the piece. (Illus. p. xvi)

trombone. A brass wind instrument with a cup-shaped mouthpiece, and a U-shaped sliding tube that is moved back and forth by the player. The movement of the tube produces the notes of the scale, in a tone that is fuller and deeper than the trumpet's. The *trombone* was invented in the 15th century and is now used by dance bands as well as symphony orchestras. There are three *trombones* in a full symphony orchestra.

troppo (TROP-poe, Italian). Too much. For example, *allegro ma non troppo* means "fast but not too fast."

troubadour (TROO-bah-door, French). A poet-musician of the 12th and 13th centuries who provided music for the courts of southern France and northern Italy. Like the minnesingers of Germany, the *troubadours* were usually nobles, trained as poets and composers. In their performances they were sometimes assisted by hired minstrels or jongleurs. The theme of the *troubadour's* songs was love, almost invariably praise of a favorite lady.

trouvère (troo-VAIR). A singing poet of northern France like the troubadour of southern France.

The *trouvères* became active in the middle of the 12th century. *See* **troubadour.**

trumpet. A brass wind instrument, the "head man" of the brass choir in a symphony orchestra. The *trumpet* has a cup-shaped mouth-

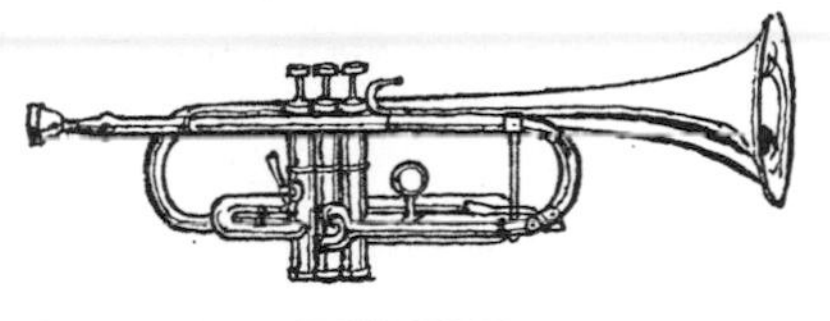

TRUMPET

piece, three valves, and a slide. It is pitched in B♭ and has a range of two and a half octaves. There are three *trumpets* in a full symphony orchestra and the instrument is also used in jazz bands. Louis Armstrong is a famous jazz *trumpet* player.

tuba. The lowest of the brass wind instruments, sometimes called the

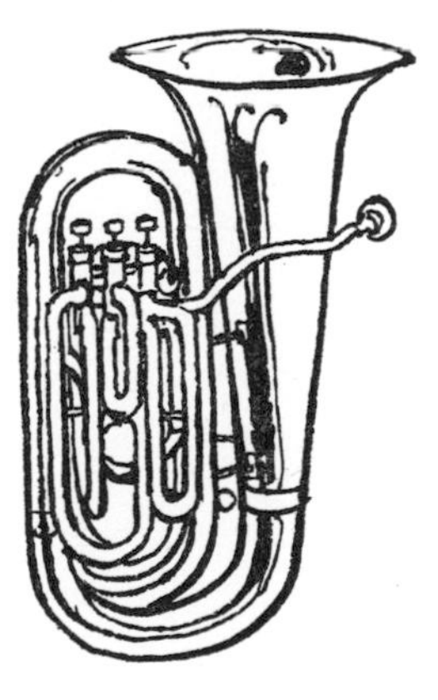

TUBA

bass tuba. In shape the instrument is something like the trumpet, although it is much larger and has the conical bore of a horn. The *tuba* has three to five valves and a cup-shaped mouthpiece. Its range is four octaves. One *tuba* is usually included in a symphony orchestra.

tune. 1. A melody. 2. To *tune* an instrument means to put it in the proper pitch. 3. *In tune* means that the pitch of one instrument or voice exactly matches the pitch of another instrument or voice.

tuning fork. A U-shaped piece of steel with a small stem at the bottom by which it is held. When

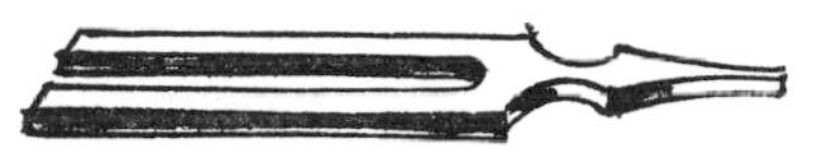

TUNING FORK

struck against a hard surface it gives an exact pitch to which a voice or instrument may be tuned. It produces an almost pure sound without overtones. The *tuning fork* was invented in 1711 by John Shore, an Englishman who was a sergeant trumpeter to George I of England.

turn. A musical ornament consisting of four notes sung or played very quickly. In some *turns,* you start at the main note, go up, then back again through the main note, down a note, and finally back again to the main note. In others, you start at the main note, go down, then back. There are a number of other arrangements of notes, also called *turns.*

tutti (TOOT-tee, Italian, "all"). The entire orchestra. Used most often in concertos to indicate that the whole orchestra resumes playing as a group, after the soloist.

tyrolienne (tee-ROH-lee-en, French). An Austro-Hungarian 19th-century dance-song in 3/4 time which combines the slow, graceful Austrian waltz with a special form of falsetto singing called "yodeling." *See* **yodeler.**

U

Über (OO-ber, German). Over. Above.

ukulele. A popular stringed instrument that looks like a small guitar. Originally from Portugal, it was brought to Hawaii in 1870.

UKULELE

It has four strings tuned to G, C, E, and A, a fretted finger board, and is played as an accompaniment for singing.

umore (oo-MORE-eh, Italian). Humor. *Con umore* is an instruction to play with humor or with a feeling of fun.

una corda (OO-nah CORD-ah, Italian). One string. As a sign, it means to use the soft, or left, pedal on the piano. This shifts the hammers under the string so that only one string vibrates to produce each tone instead of two or three strings. (*abbrev.* u.c.)

unison. 1. Performers singing or playing the same melody at the same time are *in unison.* 2. When singers or instruments are all at the same pitch, they are said to be *in unison.*

uno (OO-noe, Italian). One. Example: *Una corda* means "one string."

unruhig (oon-ROO-ig, German). Play or sing in a restless or impatient manner.

unter (OON-ter, German). Under. Below.

upbeat. 1. The sign a conductor gives to the orchestra to start playing. He raises his hand as if to say, "get ready to start." 2. A note or group of notes written on a weak beat which begins a phrase just before the first bar line.

up-bow. A direction for violinists. The bow is to be pushed over the string from its tip to the frog at its bottom. (Illus. p. xvi)

V

valse (French). A waltz. *See* **waltz.**

variation. The technique with which a melody (or theme) is presented in various arrangements. *Variation* is accomplished by altering rhythm, melody, harmony, or tone color and yet keeping enough of the original theme so that it can be recognized while the *variation* is being played. A composition in which this technique is used is described as a "theme and variations." Brahms borrowed a beautiful theme of Handel's and wrote the great piano masterpiece *Brahms-Handel Variations.*

veloce (ve-LOE-chay), Italian. Play or sing with more speed.

velocissimo (vel-loh-CHEES-ee-moe, Italian). Play as fast as you can.

vibration. A back-and-forth motion such as that of a string when it is plucked, of a reed when air is forced against it, and of a drumhead when it is struck. The *vibration* produces a sound or pattern of sounds.

vibrato (vee-BRAH-toe, Italian). A technique of playing which results in a slight fluctuation in pitch and volume. A string player produces the *vibrato* effect by a shaking motion of his left wrist. A flutist achieves it by quick changes of air pressure from his mouth. A trombonist moves the instrument's slide back and forth. A trumpet player can get the *vibrato* effect by moving the instrument slightly or by lipping.

vigoroso (vee-go-ROE-soe, Italian). Play or sing with strength and energy.

viol. A family of bowed stringed instruments developed in the 15th century and widely used until the 17th century when they were replaced by the violin family. The *viol* is very similar to the violin except that it normally has six instead of four strings, its shoulders slope downward from the neck, its sound holes are C-shaped rather than F-shaped, and its tone is less brilliant. The smaller *viols* were held in the lap or on the knee when played; larger *viols* were held between the legs of the player.

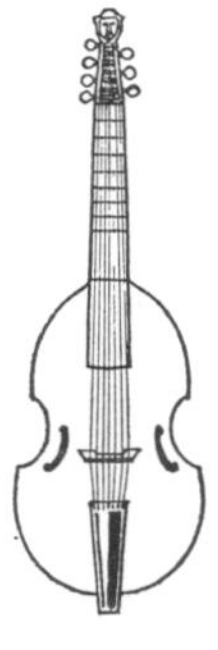

VIOL

viola (vee-o-lah, Italian). A four-stringed instrument somewhat larger than the violin, but similar in appearance and played in the same way. The *viola* has a sober and penetrating tone about a fifth

THE VIOLIN FAMILY (VIOLA, VIOLONCELLO, VIOLIN, DOUBLE BASS)

lower than the violin's. The strings are tuned to C, G, D, and A, and it has a range of about three octaves. Music for the *viola* is written on the C or alto clef. The instrument has been a member of the orchestra since the 17th century. The full symphony orchestra has about twelve *violas.* (*abbrev.* vla.)

violin. The leading stringed instrument in an orchestra and also a favorite solo instrument. The *violin* has a brilliant singing tone and has a range of over four octaves. Its strings are tuned to G, D, A, E, and its music is written in the treble clef. When played, the bottom of the *violin* is rested on the left shoulder while the left hand holds the neck in such a way that the fingers are free to curve over and stop the strings. It is played by a bow held in the right hand. The full symphony orchestra has about thirty-four *violins* (eighteen *first violins,* sixteen *second violins*). (*abbrev.* vni. for *violins* or *violini.*)

violoncello (vee-o-lon-CHEL-loe, Italian). *See* **cello.**

virginal. A small keyboard instrument similar to the harpsichord, widely used in the 16th and 17th centuries. It was shaped like an oblong box. Normally it was without legs and was placed on a table when played. The *virginal* is considered a great-grandfather of the piano. It was replaced by the spinet, which in turn was re-

VIRGINAL

placed by the harpsichord and the piano. *See* **harpsichord.**

virtuoso (ver-chew-OH-soe, Italian). A singer, dancer, or player of an instrument who performs with a brilliant technical ability.

vivace (vee-VAH-chay, Italian). Play in a lively, quick manner. (*abbrev.* viv.)

vocal. Having to do with the voice. For example *vocal* music is music written for the voice.

vocalises (voek-al-eez, French). Exercises practiced by singers to help them improve technique and tone control. Italian, French, German, and English vowel sounds are sung instead of words.

voce (VOE-chay, Italian). The voice.

voce di petto (VOE-chay dee PET-toe, Italian). The lower range of the voice—the notes which seem to be sung from the chest instead of from the head.

voce di testa (VOE-chay dee TES-tah, Italian). The upper range of the voice—the notes that seem to come from the head.

voice. The sound a person makes when singing, talking, shouting, and so forth. The human *voice* may be likened to a musical in-

VOICE RANGES

strument in which tones are produced by the vibration of the vocal chords and the resonance of the various head and throat cavities. Women's *voices* (starting with the highest) are described as soprano, mezzo-soprano, and alto (or contralto). Men's *voices,* from high to low, are classified as tenor, baritone, and bass. A young boy's *voice* is also called alto or soprano until he turns twelve or thirteen, when his *voice* usually changes and becomes lower-pitched.

voix (Vwah, French). Voice.

Volkslied (FOLKS-leet, German). Folk song.

volteggiando (vol-tej-JAHN-doe, Italian). Crossing the hands when playing on the piano keyboard.

volume. The fullness or the amount of musical sound that can be made by a voice or instrument.

vox humana (Latin). An organ reed stop that produces a sound in imitation of the human voice. *See* **stop.**

W

waltz. A dance in 3/4 time, accented on the first beat of each measure. Developed from the

WALTZ

Austrian *Ländler* dances around 1800, the *waltz* was the most popular dance in Europe in the last century, and is still popular in modern ballrooms. Many composers have written beautiful and lilting *waltzes*. Johann Strauss became known as the "Waltz King" because of the many charming *waltzes* he wrote for dancing. Chopin, Schubert, and Brahms wrote *waltzes* for the piano.

war songs. Songs associated with camp life, marching, or battles. Each nation and each army have

WAR SONGS

their favorite *war songs,* usually sung with spirit and rhythm. "Battle Hymn of the Republic," a Civil War song, and "Over There," a World War I song, are two of the American favorites.

whistle. The simplest wind instrument—really a primitive form of the flute. When it is blown, vibrations are set up which produce a sound, usually shrill. *Whistles* are made of plastic, wood, or metal.

whole note. The longest note in common use. It gets four counts in quarter time. *See* **notes and rests.**

whole rest. A sign instructing the performer to pause for a period equal in time to the length of one whole note. Also used when the composer wants an entire measure of silence, no matter what the count of the music is.

whole step. An interval equal to two half steps. A major second. The distance from one tone in a major scale to the next (except 3 and 4 and 7 and 8). On a piano keyboard, the distance between two white keys separated by a black key, or two black keys separated by a white key.

whole-tone scale. A scale which contains only whole tones. The French composer, Claude Debussy, used the *whole-tone scale* in many of his compositions. Example: C-D-E-F♯-G♯-A♯-C.

wind instruments. Musical instruments which the player blows into to produce sound. There are two classes of *wind instruments:* the woodwinds (such as the clarinet, oboe, flute, etc.) and the brasses (such as the trumpet, trombone, tuba, etc.).

woodwind choir. The woodwind instruments of an orchestra: the flute, clarinet, oboe, and bassoon, English horn, contra bassoon, bass clarinet, and sometimes the piccolo.

woodwind instruments. Wind instruments made mostly of wood. They use three kinds of mouthpieces: single-reed, double-reed, and mouth holes. The clarinet and saxophone are single-reed woodwinds. The oboe family are double-reed woodwinds. The flute has a mouth hole. Although the saxophone is made of metal and, in this country, so is the flute in most cases, both are considered woodwinds.

work songs. For centuries men and women have sung while they worked to gladden their spirits, lighten their labors, and express their sense of community. *Work songs* have come from the fields, from sailing vessels, railroads, and factories. They have been sung by cowboys, by men on canal boats, and by men building tunnels. They range in feeling from the rollicking good humor of a sea shanty like "Blow the Man Down" to the loneliness of a mournful cowboy ballad. Collectively they are a true people's art and an expression of emotions common to men everywhere. They constitute an important contribution to music.

X

xylophone. A very old percussion instrument still used in both symphony orchestras and jazz bands. It consists of a row of flat wooden blocks fastened horizontally to two stretched cords. The blocks are in graduated sizes and, like the keys of the piano, are tuned to a chromatic scale. They make a clear musical tone when struck with a wooden mallet. The instrument's compass is two octaves in the treble range.

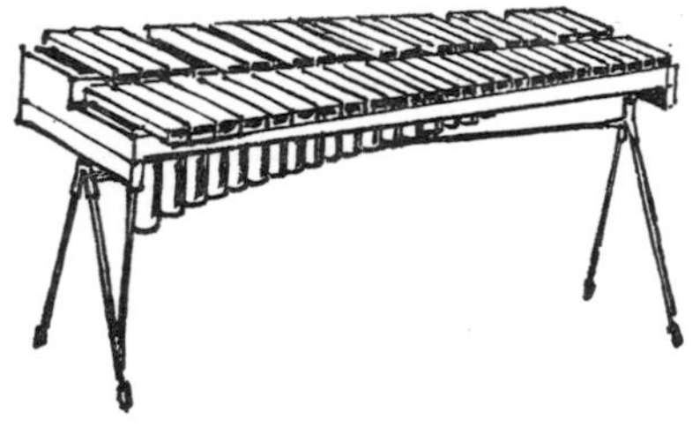

XYLOPHONE

Y

yodeler. A singer who warbles a yodel, a song produced by alternating high falsetto notes with low chest notes. Yodels originated in the Austrial Tyrol country, but are now mostly performed by singers of the Alpine country of Switzerland.

yuehchin. A Chinese guitar, also known as a "moon guitar."

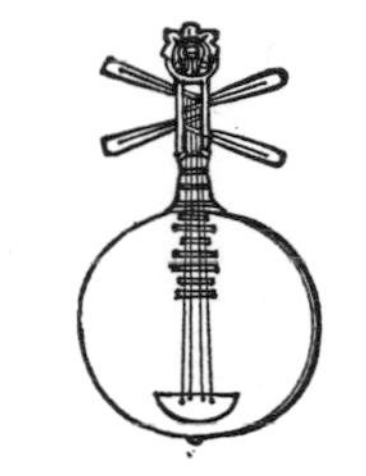

YUEHCHIN (GUITAR)

Z

zapateado (thah-pah-tay-AH-doe). A Spanish dance in 3/4 time. The dancer clicks his heels smartly throughout the dance to mark the beat of the music against the rhythm of the accompaniment.

zither. A stringed instrument popular in Austria consisting of a shallow, oblong, wooden sound box over which from thirty to thirty-six strings are stretched. The main melody is played on five strings (known as the "melody strings") which lie over a fretted finger board. These strings are stopped by the left-hand thumb while they are being played by a plectrum (or metal ring) attached to the right-hand thumb. The other fingers of the right hand pluck an accompaniment on the remaining strings.

ZITHER